the COMEBACK

the COMEBACK
HOW TO WIN AGAINST ALL ODDS

DEE EDWARDS
and 14 Courageous Women

THE COMEBACK
Published by Purposely Created Publishing Group™
Copyright © 2018 Dee Edwards

All rights reserved.

No part of this book may be reproduced, distributed or transmitted in any form by any means, graphics, electronics, or mechanical, including photocopy, recording, taping, or by any information storage or retrieval system, without permission in writing from the publisher, except in the case of reprints in the context of reviews, quotes, or references.

Scriptures marked AMP are taken from the Amplified Version®. Copyright © 2015 by The Lockman Foundation. All rights reserved.

Scriptures marked TLB are taken from The Living Bible copyright © 1971 by Tyndale House Foundation. Used by permission of Tyndale House Publishers Inc., Carol Stream, Illinois 60188.

Printed in the United States of America

ISBN: 978-1-947054-90-5

Special discounts are available on bulk quantity purchases by book clubs, associations and special interest groups. For details email: sales@publishyourgift.com or call (888) 949-6228.

For information logon to:
www.PublishYourGift.com

DEDICATION

I dedicate this book to the courageous women who decided to help others bounce back and make it through their storms. Thank you for your transparency, openness, willingness, and time to assist others understand that their comebacks are going to be greater than anything they have ever experienced. I celebrate your comeback and speak well over your future. May you be strengthened again and healed from the words you have written in this book.

God bless you and all your endeavors.

Dee Edwards

TABLE OF CONTENTS

Foreword 1

Introduction 3

Remember to Forget 7
Mary Mallory

Faithless Warrior 15
Shan Washington

Hidden Truth Exposed 23
Melissa Williams

From Riches to Rags 33
Jamika Mays

The Waiting Room 43
Victoria Necole

Breaking Cycles 53
Mesia Rena

My Ugliest Beautiful 63
Terria R. Jones

The Art of Partnership 71
Starnisha Washington

Beyond Broke and Loving What I Do 81
Nicole Johnson

Reaching Out to Give a Hand Up 89
Geonisha Brown

Get Out of Your Own Way 97
Stacey Yvonne

The Palm Tree Effect 105
Crystal M. NeVille

Relax and Reset 113
Cynthia E. Rodgers

After Tragedy Comes Triumph 121
Katrina Seals

Your Latter Can Be Greater Than Your Former Years . . . 129
Dee Edwards

About the Authors 139

FOREWORD

By the age of thirteen, I had already recorded my first album, traveled and opened for the likes of Stevie Wonder, B.B. King, and Aretha Franklin, and became a national recording artist and Grammy nominee. But everything that glitters isn't gold. Although I had creativity and talent, I, from a young age, was exposed to a lot of grown men in nightclubs and show. I started living for fame and fortune, loving the spotlight while seeking fulfillment separate from God's original intent and plan for my life.

The vulnerable six-year-old girl in me who was molested and violated sought to fill the void of her parent's abandonment through trading her body for affection. I honestly thought it was true love to have a child out of wedlock at sixteen. By eighteen, I was strung out on drugs and cocaine became my best friend. I was forced to sell my body and use my sexuality to fulfill my psychological and emotional needs.

Though I often wondered if God was mad at me, I always felt His hands over me. Even after losing everything, He delivered me: I was born again and married, and am now recording again, traveling the world to share my testimony. Don't lose hope. Your faith in the storm will reap new rewards. The odds may be against you today, but stand flat-footed and trust Him.

Your mind is the battlefield of your faith and, if things are going to change in your life, start with your thought pattern. Philippians 4:8 says, "Finally, brethren, whatsoever things are true, whatsoever things are honest, whatsoever things are just, whatsoever things are pure, whatsoever things are lovely, whatsoever things are of good report; if there be any virtue, and if there be any praise, think on these things." No matter what you go through, seek God for wisdom, ask Him to lead you to the right people and church, and spend time in prayer to feed your faith.

This book was written by women who boldly share their raw, uncut truth for the sake of helping you understand that God will turn your pain into your promise. He will position you for the greatest comeback of your life.

Dr. Helen Baylor
Dove Award Winner, Multiple Grammy-Nominated Recording Artist

INTRODUCTION

If you have dealt with financial issues, business failure, rejection, abandonment, hatred, depression, loneliness, anger, shame, and guilt, and have lost yourself in the process, so have we, the authors of this book. We share our truths, the ugliest and most embarrassing times of our lives, with the hope of bringing healing to every reader who feels stuck, alone, and abandoned. Although we have gone through different circumstances, we have different upbringings; we are different shapes, sizes, and ages; we have one commonality: we've all been on the verge of giving up.

We made choices and decisions that left us feeling hopeless. We had things happen to us that we would not wish on our worst enemy. We lost our minds, our innocence, our marriages, our children, our parents, and our businesses, and became victims to the voices in our heads. They surrounded and tormented us day and night, ripping away our confidence. We were left with emotional baggage, mental anguish, bad dreams, debt, low self-esteem, and resentment. Life seemed unfair. It was hard to understand that bad things happen to good people. But now we know that we had to go through the valley in order to appreciate the mountaintop. We had to go through it for you. The valleys in our lives built our endurance, character, resilience, and tenacity, while also revealing other people's truest intents and motives. Sometimes, you must be taken to the lowest place in order to see your circumstance from another perspective.

This is called your process. It doesn't make sense. It doesn't feel good. It's hard to understand. It's hard to get up every day and go to work, run a business, take care of kids and other family members when you've cried yourself to sleep the night before. You've stood firm on a promise that still hasn't been fulfilled. But after reading our personal journeys, you will understand that you can win against all odds. That which happened to you or what you may be experiencing is not the end. Your setback can be the greatest comeback of your life if you allow it to work for your good.

A comeback is to recover from deficit. While in the storm, you may not see how all of what you are going through is working for your good. But neither did Job in the Bible who received double for his trouble. Neither did Steve Harvey, Shaquille O'Neal, or the authors of this book. It's usually the individuals born into adverse conditions, faced with disadvantageous situations, or deemed the black sheep of the family who end up being the most successful.

In life, you are going to be faced with two dilemmas: a dream that is bigger than you and adversity. Initially, both seem too overwhelming, so the average person gives up. However, the key is being able to use what you've been through as lessons to draw you closer to the dream. We believe that after reading *The Comeback*, you will find exactly what you need to gain composure again. You will spring forth and position yourself to recover from what you thought was going to get the best of you. It's not over yet. You still have time to win against all odds.

This is your year of the comeback.

REMEMBER TO FORGET

Mary Mallory

Some say, "Don't forget where you came from." But some things are just not worth remembering! I grew up with my mother, six brothers, and one sister in a three-bedroom house. I had a loving family who didn't always have a lot of material things, but we had love and one another. But even with all these people in the house, I sometimes felt like I was alone. It wasn't the fact that I was left out or mistreated: I had the normal sibling rivalries and was teased as the butt of loving jokes, especially during the Christmas holiday. But I still felt distant from others.

My siblings and I spent time playing cards and all types of games we would make up. We would roll in large truck tires and played school when we helped each other with homework. One of my favorites was the talent show. We would each chose a song and dance, and sometimes spend all night singing, dancing, and laughing. Once, I laughed so hard that I threw up all over the place, and my siblings called me Ms. Puke for the rest of the night.

But there was one song, "The Man is Down on Me," I always absolutely hated to hear. It made me feel so weird and uncomfortable and I didn't know why. All I knew was that the record reminded me of someone touching me in places that made me feel bad. I couldn't figure out if it was something that actually happened or if it was all just a dream because the touching always happened during bedtime. But if it was a dream, why did I have the same one with the same person every night? And why did I hurt the next morning? I prayed for the memory to go away and sure enough it stopped. I forgot about it.

I loved going to school. I did well and was often at the top in my classes. There were times when my classmates made me feel bad. They made fun of my clothes since I didn't have the best of things, mostly just hand-me-downs. So, to get away, I helped the teachers or worked in the office. I loved the fact that I could feel needed.

After finishing school, I found jobs that would allow me to interact with people. I was a data processing clerk, a receptionist, and even a physician assistant at a Women's Clinic. I truly enjoyed being in position where I could make people feel comfortable and get through some of their most difficult times. While working at the women's clinic, I began to draw nearer to God. I soon started working at the church kindergarten and summer camp. This was rewarding because, once again, I was helping to plant a positive seed into the lives of young people. My life was also blessed with a marriage and a family.

One day I got up, dressed, and went to work with the kids. The day started out as usual and, during naptime, my coworker and I began to talk about the latest news and everything else that was going on in our lives. All of a sudden, she steered the conversation in a different direction. She talked about sexual abuse and how it was important for us to protect and keep our young girls safe from sexual predators. Then she said, "I wouldn't want what happened to me to happen to any of them. I was touched inappropriately when I was a little girl. I didn't know how to tell anyone." I immediately stopped talking and just listened. She continued, "It was a family member and he was grown too. He shouldn't have done that to me. He knew it was wrong."

As she kept talking, I felt uneasy. I thought and remembered what I had "forgotten:" it happened to me too. Then before I knew it, I blurted out, "I know because it happened to me." I stopped in my tracks. Hey, who just said that? Did I just say that? I had never shared that experience with anyone, not even myself.

I didn't say much more after that, but I allowed my mind to remember what I went through in the past. The conversation seemed to last forever and I wished she would stop talking. Finally, it was time to get the children up from their naps to give them their snacks and prepare them to go home. I was relieved and thought that, if I get back to work, I would forget about those memories. But that conversation was all I could think about for the rest of the day.

When I went home, the memories were still on my mind and all through the night. I remembered all the ugly details vividly, as if they were happening all over again. All the uncomfortable, hurtful, shameful, and guilty feelings surfaced. It was hard for me to have a conversation with my husband and my children. I asked myself, "Why now? Why did it come back up? What was I going to do?" I was filled with disturbing thoughts of my worst memories and it consumed every quiet moment. It was hard for me to bring myself to say that I had been molested as a child, no less mention the word "rape." Yes, I had been raped!

My thoughts began to affect my relationship with my husband. It was difficult for me to be intimate with him and not think of what had happened. I thought that I had buried that part of my life and I didn't want to remember it now. But I was overwhelmed with shame and guilt. I felt sad, I felt angry, and I felt unwanted like damaged goods. Every move I made, every situation I encountered brought me back to that place in the past.

I started to question the things that had happened in my life. I felt like a different person in my behavior as it took control of how I socialized with people. I didn't want to be around others since I felt like everyone knew and was judging me for what happened. Maybe I was wrong to think that I was as good as anyone else. I would ask myself, "Why did that happen to me? Is that the reason I was teased? Is that why certain people didn't like me? Is that why I act so different from others?" I wanted to hide. I found myself crying at the drop of a hat. I stopped leaving the house unless it was necessary or to go to church. Sometimes, I didn't even want to go to church because I felt like a hypocrite with my secret.

When I absolutely had to go out around others, I put on my mask with a big smile. I learned to act like everything was all right but I was miserable. I was slowing dying on the inside. As a matter of fact, I thought about driving off the road, down a cliff, and ending my life to stop the pain I was experiencing. The only thing that prevented me was the thought that I might not succeed and be left in a state that would require others to take care of me—and I didn't think anyone loved me enough to take care of me. My thoughts were all over the place. I started staying in bed all day but I couldn't sleep. I started drinking to numb the pain and would drink myself to sleep at night. After a while, that was my normal daily activity.

One day, as I passed the mirror, I didn't recognize the person looking back at me. I hated who I had become. My situation was beyond me and I needed some help. I prayed and cried out to God, day in and day out. My general doctor suggested that I seek a psychiatrist and gave me a referral. After the psychiatrist examined me, I was diagnosed with depression and anxiety. He prescribed pills for the depression, pills to stay alert, and pills to sleep. I was a walking zombie. Now, not only did I have my past haunting me, deciding what I did, where I went, who I talked to, and what I said, I also had to take drugs to get through the day. My behavior spiraled out of control. I did things that were out of my character and I was not the same person.

I needed someone trusted to talk to about what I was going through. I cried out to Jesus! I prayed more than ever and talked to Him. One day, while driving to the doctor's office with tears in my eyes, my prayers were answered. I heard a voice say, "I love you and I hear you." It was so loud that I thought someone was in the car with me. Yes, God told me that He knew all I had been through. He reminded me He was there all the time and He had kept me by helping me forget the past in order to overcome that time. He told me I was His child and He forgives me for the things that I had done in my time of pain. Now, it was time for me to forgive myself and those who had wronged me. He reminded me of this scripture: "Brothers and sisters, I do not consider myself yet to have taken hold of it. But one thing I do: Forgetting what is behind and straining toward what is ahead, I press on toward the goal to win the prize for which God has called me heavenward in Christ Jesus" (Philippians 3:13-14 NIV). I wasn't sure how I was going to achieve my salvation but I knew I could trust God to help me to do it.

When I reached the doctor's office, I was assigned a therapist chosen by God. She sympathized with me and ministered to me to help strengthen my faith in God. I recognized His sudden works. I learned to work through my circumstances and began to see who I was in the eyes of God. I was reminded that it was good that I had forgotten my past because it did not define who I am today. Before, I had been convinced that my hardships were meant to place me in prison and prevent me from moving forward to accomplish the things that I was to do in the future. I now had to learn from those moments, forget, and move on.

I did assignments by reading and meditating on certain scriptures in the Bible. I colored in a coloring book and journaled, which gave me a different outlook on where I had come and how much I had accomplished in my life. I was a great wife and mother, a committed church member, and a loyal family member and friend. I realized I was a successful, caring, compassionate, and strong woman. I was wonderfully and fearfully made as stated in Psalm 139:14. I believed Jeremiah 29:11: "God knows the plans he has planned for you, to prosper and not to be harmed, plans to give you hope and a future." That was for me too!

I'm grateful I read, listened, and obeyed the words of God. They helped me to pull myself together and get out of bed and the house. Soon, I began dressing every day even if I didn't have anywhere to go. I took time to put on my makeup. I changed my hairstyle to enhance the uniqueness I possessed. I now know that I was not created to be like anybody else—I have my own qualities and abilities.

Today, I embrace who I am and make my contribution to the world. I'm not only reading the Bible, but I'm also studying it and have graduated Bible College with a bachelor of arts in pastoral studies. I'm striving to move forward to perform the things that have already been ordained for my life. I'm living in my present and preparing for my future.

So, if you are struggling because you've been mentally, physically, or sexually abused or because you have experienced pain and hurt in your past, I encourage you to remember to forget! Forgive and forget the perpetrators, and forgive yourself. Be thankful to God that you lived through the trauma and that you are here today. Don't be afraid to seek help from a professional, if you need it. Remember that you are beautiful. You are created to be a positive influence and that's why the enemy doesn't want you to complete your mission. What you endured was not for you but a testimony to be used for the benefit of others you will encounter. If you choose to, you can win against all odds.

Father God, I thank You for each day of our lives, the good and the bad. I ask that those who are reading this will find strength in knowing that You are always with us. I pray they will use my story to obtain hope for any situation they may be facing, to know that You will do the same for them. Father, I ask You to meet them at their need and heal the hurt. Help them to forgive themselves and others. I pray that they use their past experiences to become a voice of healing, for themselves and others alike. Father, I ask that You give them power over the enemy. We thank and praise You in advance.

In the matchless, powerfully name of Jesus and for His Glory. Amen

FAITHLESS WARRIOR
Fighting with an Incarcerated Heart

Shan Washington

An ambitious, kind, hardworking, and loving mother—she carries the weight of the world on her every day. She continues to neglect herself and her well-being for everything else. She loves God, but wonders why she is going through so much pain and hurt. What is she being punished for?

She has had some awesome life events, but one major hit in her journey caused a lifetime of pain. She was once a courageous, beautiful girl with the potential for success and the determination to do what she wanted. It's strange how one single day can be the start of a downward storm, turning those positive feelings to the total opposite. But through all the pain, she still got up every day. She never got over her trauma, but she learned who the war really belonged to. I know her story all too well because I am this mother. "She" is me.

The year of 2012 was the start of a storm in my life. Earlier in that year, I discovered that I was expecting my second born, a baby boy, who I wanted so dearly. He was to come into the world and complete our family, along with my daughter, Zuri, and my fiancé, TP. But soon, we experienced a financial hit that shook us to the core. Already emotional from my pregnancy, that hit sent me into a deep depression. TP did the best he knew how at the time to ensure that we could stay afloat. He also tried his best to remain positive and played the role well. But, I knew he was uncomfortable. I didn't think our situation could not get any worse.

Still, as I got closer to my delivery date, I grew happier and more positive. I was determined to birth my child into a happy atmosphere. Plus, I had my daughter for whom I needed to stay positive. My baby boy, Zane, arrived on November 1st, a day I will never forget. But little did I know that another day in that month would soon be memorialized. My life would be robbed. More importantly, my family would be robbed.

The morning of November 29th, I sat on the side of my bed, dressing our daughter for school, as TP lay in bed feeding our son. All three of us were happily singing "Happy Birthday" to Zane since that day he had turned four-weeks-old! My life was on a natural high that I didn't want to give up. I had a man who I loved so much, a beautiful daughter, and a handsome son. I had just finished dressing Zuri when I heard someone at the door. We weren't expecting anyone that early in the morning, so I was immediately alarmed. TP laid the baby down to see what was going on at the door. Before we could realize what was happening, the home alarm system went off. They were already inside.

I didn't know who they were or what they wanted. All I knew is that I wanted my kids safe. As I began to hide them under the bed, I heard from a distance: "Police! It's the US Marshals! Nobody move." I felt my heart fall to the floor. I couldn't breathe, move, or process quickly enough what was happening. These rude men with big guns were in my home, searching for my love, my kids' father. They punched, kicked, and beat on him, and there was nothing that I could do. Our daughter was begging for them to stop because she could hear his groans of pain.

As they took him away through the door that they tore down, a chunk of me left too. Someone had pressed pause on my life and on my family's plans. I was to later find out that he was being accused of being an accomplice in a burglary and home invasion. I was completely taken aback by these accusations—why would TP do such a thing? The crimes did not match the man I knew and had a relationship with. So many thoughts raced through my head, so many emotions destroyed my heart. At that moment, the storm began.

Because I suddenly became a single mother of two, I had to immediately start working. Our kids were no longer a part of a "two-parent" household. Depression had a hold on me so tight that I could no longer produce milk to feed my child, and I became a lifeless shell. Every day, my kids gave me the power and motivation to fight another twenty-four hours, but I was losing faith on having positive a future. Sadly, I also began to lose faith in God. Although I made the decision to stay loyal to TP and be supportive during his time in prison, my heart and life were soon placed behind bars as well.

Little by little I started to change, and not for the better. I locked myself in; if I wasn't going to work or taking the kids to school, I was at home. I no longer wanted to travel or spend time with my friends, and the more time I spent at home, the more I slept. I even spent less time with my kids. Part of me didn't want to be out because I didn't want to face the questions that I knew people were going to ask. "What happened?" "How is he?" "How are the kids?" "How are you?" I didn't want to answer those questions at all. I didn't want it to be real. I couldn't face the fact that my life had flipped and spiraled out of control.

But as much as I tried to ignore and not talk about what happened, the trauma and pain started to show in my behavior. See, the depression was only the beginning of the onslaught of bad feelings and emotions. It started from the inside; my confidence and self-esteem were at an all-time low. I gained so much weight that I couldn't fit into any of my clothes. I stopped my regular routine of going to the salon and the spa, and did nothing with myself aside from taking care of basic hygiene. The high-spirited Shan was gone. I was not myself. My "happy glow" was nowhere to be found in the mirror. It took everything in me to get up every day and still go on with my life and responsibilities.

I didn't realize it then, but I was fighting a battle in which I had no power to fight. Every time I attempted to take on a circumstance, I had to cut off a piece of myself because I was not prepared. I was going to war without my proper tools: faith and God. My prayers were minimal before they stopped altogether. I lost my grip on my foundation. In my heart, I knew God was my Father and that I needed Him, but I felt like He was no longer hearing me. I thought He was disappointed in me and had let me go.

Here I was, alone in the wilderness, mind and body full of war wounds, no strength or tools to fight. The changes in my behavior were cries for help, but no one was listening. My family heard me, but they were not *listening*. They knew I was stressed, but they assumed that it would eventually pass and that I would be just fine. In my heart, I feel that their insensitivity was not intentional. I have always had a naturally strong spirit and personality, so they felt that I could handle it. But little did they know that I had given up. I was too weak to fight.

It got to a point where my daughter could constantly see the pain in my face and attitude and would always ask if I was okay. One day, she heard me crying, which had become a daily ritual. I tried to reassure her that we'd be fine, but that was when she said something that shook me in the inside. She said, "Don't worry, mommy. I will help you take care of my brother."

The fact that my child felt the need to help me out of my sadness was enough! I knew then that I had to do something. I could no longer sit and waddle in pity. I let depression and stress take control over my life for four years, and now I was tired. Tired of being an empty soul. Tired of being a walking robot. Tired of just existing and not living. I was just plain exhausted!

I had to accept the fact that I could not change what had happened to us. I could only make the best of the situation that we were in. Yes, our lives had been interrupted. Yes, my children's father was incarcerated, but I didn't have to be. I began to forgive myself for giving up on God and blaming Him for my troubles. I began faithfully praying again, and I let Him lead me. I realized that, although my kids' biological father was gone temporarily, God, *The* Father, was all we needed.

After I started to slowly get back to my true self, everything else fell in line. I began to live a less confrontational life and took a big leap of faith with my business. In April of 2017, I joined a business venture that is now an umbrella to what are now my two businesses. It was a huge start for everything that my family and I needed for the future. Although my situation didn't change, I had to change the way I viewed life.

In life, we all go through things that cannot be controlled by our own selves, but we must never let those challenges take over how we carry and treat ourselves. During my heart-aching experience, I hated myself. I hated how I let depression steal my joy, my happiness, my love for myself, and my time. I let it control my life instead of using my experience to get closer to God.

When bad things happen, it's okay to feel anger, hurt, disappointment, and more. But, never let it get you so off focus that you forget what you were built on. Throwing away the love you have for yourself is not part of the process. Storms make us stronger for the next level that God wants to bless us with. How we approach the situation and pass the test are up to us. God wants to know just how much we trust Him and His process. If you continue going to war unequipped and without Him in the forefront, you will lose. You are not ready for the next level.

My situation took me down into the valley, but when I started to realize the "why" behind my story, I became clearer on what I needed to do. Every hurdle I jumped, every stone thrown at me, every desire and dream that I yearned for—they all contributed to my accomplishments today. I now know that my sacrifices are my testimony to help and encourage others. My circumstances were not in vain. I learned that I can win against all odds.

The tools to win the war were always inside of me—God and faith! They're the reason for my comeback.

HIDDEN TRUTH EXPOSED

Melissa Williams

It was one of the most beautiful, exciting days of my life. I was at home, preparing for a speaking engagement for the Mary Kay's Business Success Empowerment Seminar. This conference was an opportunity for me to operate in a different light outside of the walls of a church ministry. For two years in a row, I'd been asked to be the guest speaker, and what a privilege it was to finally be able to say yes!

As I studied my prepared speech, I began to listen to a worship song and pray, asking the Father to be with me, guide me, and speak through me. But there was something going on within me that I had to admit. I'd been feeling lost, somewhat unbalanced, and uncertain. My prayer was "Lord, I need You to make things clear to me."

Often times, we find ourselves operating in a capacity that reveals our gifts and talents but also leaves us feeling unfulfilled. We feel like we've accomplished some level of success in a particular field, then we stop there, never to venture or question, "Is there more?" I too was at the crossroads of analyzing if there was more to my life than where I was. Yes, I was traveling all across the country and my life was rewarding, but something was missing. I had only questions and no answers. Even though this speaking engagement was huge and I absolutely loved what I did, I needed to know: is this it? Am I really following the path He has preordained for me?

In the restroom, I put my makeup on and got ready. That was when I heard a still voice in my spirit: "If you tap into who you are, you will tap into where you're supposed to be."

Did I just hear that? Did the Holy Spirit just say this to me? I was in awe. I quickly ran to my bedroom to grab my journal and I began to cry. The tears started to stream down my face and, instantly, I said in a whisper, "Show me."

I arrived at the convention center and was greeted at the doors by the host and her assistant. I was escorted to the green room to meditate. Shortly after, I told them that I was ready and then I was escorted into a room full of successful, beautiful black women. They applauded me as I embraced the vibrant energy in the room. It was overwhelming being welcomed by women who were executives, CEOs, single mothers, and wives. These were women who were ready to achieve and build, and every last one of them was waiting to hear from me. No pressure, right?

As I sat there going over my speech for the final time, I heard that still voice again say, "If you tap into who you are, you will tap into where you're supposed to be." Then I heard Him say, "Trust me." I paused and pondered. With the words replaying in my head, I took a breath and walked out on stage. When I opened my mouth, everything that I had prepared to say no longer seemed to matter. I allowed what was in me to give life.

Life is our one common denominator. Some days, it's a merry-go-round and, other days, it's a roller coaster. The fact remains that we are all on its mysterious tracks and we pray it leads us to beauty, health, happiness, success, prosperity, and love. Never do we embrace our day-to-day life expecting the worse. No, we should greet each day with great anticipation of the wonderful things we believe will happen for us. Unfortunately, there are times that life compels us to stop in our tracks. It is this form of interruption that opens our eyes and makes us see that nothing stays the same. We either reveal our greatest strengths or fall to vulnerability and weakness. It is experiences such as these that qualify us for a comeback. While traveling your journey, one day you may be celebrating and the next day you may be reliving the worst moments of your life.

Monday, June 12, 2017, was the day I was awakened. I had just spent a weekend in Capitol Heights, Maryland where I had been invited to preach the 18th Pastoral and Church Anniversary Revival for a very dear friend of mine, and I was now returning home. As our flight landed in our city, my assistant and I were both tired but excited to be back in our element.

Returning home, all I wanted to do was to get in my bed and get lost under the covers. A few hours later, my phone began to ring. It was five in the morning. I thought to myself, "Stay asleep, Melissa. They will call back later!" Well the ring stopped, only to start ringing again. I looked to see who it was and the caller ID displayed the number for the childcare center I owned.

My childcare director's voice said calmly, "Ms. Melissa, I'm so sorry to wake you. But I need you to come to the daycare." With my eyes still closed, I paused to take a deep breath because I wanted to believe I was dreaming this call. But, in my director's voice, I heard pain.

"What's going on?" I asked.

She then said in the most apologetic, terrified tone of voice I had ever heard, "Ms. Melissa, they found two dead bodies in the parking lot."

I sat straight up in the bed. I hung up the phone, threw on my clothes and a hat, and jumped into my vehicle. As I drove, I started to pray for God to be with me as I faced what was awaiting my arrival. So many things went through my mind: is it one of my families enrolled at the center? Is it my own family? Nothing could prepare me for this life-changing encounter.

I arrived at the center, which was now a crime scene. I parked to see all the police cars and the many media outlets and news reporters. I ran to the front entrance door when, in my view to my left, I saw two dead bodies in a car. My heart stopped as my legs carried me into the facility.

My director came to me in tears and said, "Ms. Melissa, look." I looked to see a black woman sitting on the sidewalk of my childcare center, crying. As I approached her, I could hear the pain in her weeping. A sound of deep hurt hat I had never heard in my life. I leaned over to this stranger, this woman I had never met before and embraced her, only to hear the words that will haunt me for life. She said to me in a shattered whisper, "That's not my baby."

I repeated, "I'm so sorry." I found myself in the middle of a tug of war between life and death, prayer and reality, the strength granted to me and the sorrow I felt. Officers soon approached us and escorted us to the car with the bodies. There, they confirmed that her daughter was deceased. The mother fell to the ground and screamed her daughter's name. Instantly, my heart pricked: the name of her nineteen-year-old daughter who had just been murdered by her boyfriend was the same one as my oldest daughter's.

We were no longer strangers in passing. She had become a siren of reminders, a sound of awakening fears. This alarm resurfaced a part of my life that I had made myself forget about. What had become a distant memory was now a present thought.

My hidden truth was now looking at me: broken nose, fractured jaw, broken teeth, gashed tongue, gash above my right cheek that required thirty-two stitches. To this day, I have little feeling on two of my fingers on my left hand, a result of me grabbing the butcher knife my abuser tried to use to cut my throat with. After the beating, he left me for three days to die. Why me? How did I choose someone like him? Why did he beat me like this? I thought he loved me.

Many times, we don't have the privilege to choose our hurts or disappointments. Forest Gump's mother said, "Life is like a box of chocolate. You never know what you'll get." Well, my life was like a chocolate factory. Life as I knew it was hell.

Have you ever gone through so much that it feels like you'll never get a break? You never really find a sense of purpose and you never adapt to happiness because it's foreign. I have always had to live my life like I was stronger than anything or anyone who knew me. I've had to hold my head up high in front of others, just to go behind closed doors to cry. I'm so grateful to God that He saw the best in me when others saw the worst. I'm so happy that the most detrimental situations in my life have made me someone who knows she can survive the enemy's attacks. I am an example of how the Lord will use a mess to create a miracle.

I am a survivor of domestic violence. I am an advocate for forgiveness. I am an example of the word of God being revealed. I am evidence that, when God has a plan for your life, it doesn't matter where you start, it matters where you end. My start was brutal but my today is beautiful. I've gone from living life in regret and shame to sharing my testimony with millions. I am the face of joy when pain has to pay you back.

After many years of dealing with the aftermath of the abuse, I've had to train myself to look in the mirror and be okay. Every time someone looks you in the face, you wonder if they are looking at your scars. I've had to live past the scars, the memories, the nightmares, and the bodily pains that come from such abuse. I've had to overcome the failures of my short-term memory after taking multiple blows to the skull. I now understand that my history will not stop or dictate my destiny. It actually qualifies me to continue to become who I choose to be.

Today, I live a life as a world-renowned Evangelist, author, and entrepreneur whom the Lord has graced to travel the country to preach His word. I have the honor of speaking to millions of men and women at seminars and conferences and helping others through my mentorship program. I'm often asked how I made it out and I know that my path to my healing started with one word: forgiveness. I had to be taught to forgive everybody. I had to forgive the person who left me for dead. I had to forgive the person who betrayed me and caused me a life of realities that others don't know I live with daily. But forgiveness for me is the blessing that keeps on giving, because it releases me from the control of shame and fear. It's a powerful tool but an even greater weapon. It's the power to live.

Forgiveness for some does not happen overnight, but it is a process. I will never forget the moment I knew I had arrived at the destination of healing. It was the moment of truth, standing face to face with the giant in my life. I looked at my abuser in the eyes and I didn't want to kill him. Instead, I began to pray for the deliverance of his soul. I told him, "I forgive you." At that moment, I had such a peace.

It is my prayer that, regardless of whatever cards life has dealt you, you will not allow it to stop you from living on purpose. The trials you live past will be the very thing that equips and empowers you to continue to be a successful person. Allow what caused you pain to identify your purpose. It's through the pains of life that victory feels so good! It's after you've suffered that the highs of your tomorrow mean so much more. Never make the pain of your life the limit of your life. If so, you will miss the purpose for which you were born. Life's experiences are meant to thrust you towards your takeoff, teach you how to soar above what stagnate others on the runway, and clearly open your eyes for the path ahead.

I know I was born for this. If I had not lived through it all, I wouldn't know my own strength. If I had not faced the pain of the abuse, I wouldn't know how to celebrate everyday with people who love me. *Life is always a reminder that you're alive.* Whether life is introducing you to another blow or another accomplishment, allow the plan of God to lead the way and introduce you to what you were born to do. Even if you learn it while fighting through tears and asking Him, "Why me?" there is nothing that can stop you. You are who you are by the grace of God, and it's through Him that you shall become what you believe.

Start living your life on purpose. People you thought you'd never connect with will take you to places you'd only dreamed of. I'm not telling you something I've heard. This is the life I've lived. Welcome to freedom in forgiveness. This is the year of your comeback.

FROM RICHES TO RAGS
My Cinderella Story

....

Jamika Mays

I was my mother's first child and my daddy's baby, literally the first child of the household. I was a daddy's girl. He spoiled me and, being born to the most loving parents, I was destined to make it and be great. That is until the storms started to rage in my life. When I turned eight-months-old, my dad was sentenced to life in prison without parole. My dad wanted my grandmother Dear to raise me, so she legally adopted me as her own. I grew up with everything and never wanted for anything. Dear picked off where my dad left off.

Since I was used to getting everything I wanted, I was a spoil brat. I wanted what I wanted when I wanted it. I didn't understand the value of a dollar. I literally thought money grew on trees. I grew up in a non-traditional household with my grandmother, my aunt (my grandma's only daughter and my daddy's only sister), and my cousin (my aunt's only child) who hated me from the start. My cousin thought I was favored since Dear had a love for me like no other. I'm sure she felt threatened and rejected but I didn't see it like that at first. I couldn't understand why my cousin would treat me so badly and be so mean to me.

I went to the best schools, first attending the AOH Cathedral early age program and then pre-K at St. Paul Cathedral in downtown Birmingham, Alabama. I went there until fifth grade, only because I pitched a fit for Dear to let me go to regular school so I wouldn't have to wear uniforms. I always got what I wanted, so in sixth grade, I attended Tarrant Middle School.

While most people thought I had everything, there was still something missing in my life. Material things could no longer fill its void. Around eight-years-old, I started to realize that I didn't have my mom or dad. I had all the stuff, but others had what I wanted: parents. Kids at school started asking me about my mom and dad and why I was always with my grandma. I would tell them my dad was in prison and that my grandma took me to see him every single weekend since he was incarcerated, even if she had to pay somebody to take us. But the questions as to why I wasn't with my mom were left unanswered and that made me sad.

There were times that one of my cousins would come get me for a little while and then ask me if I wanted to go see my mom. Of course, I would always say yes, and she would take me around where my mom was, but never for very long.

Then, when Dear found out about our outings, she forbid my cousin from taking me with her again. Still, she would sneak me out on occasions, making me promise that I wouldn't tell.

I've always been inquisitive and curious about things. I would ask question after questions until I got my answer. I probably knew more than I should for my age so I knew how to keep a promise. Soon, I realized that if I acted like I didn't hear a word around people, they would continue talking around me and I'd gain valuable insight. One day, I was sitting around some grown people who were talking about my family and how my mom didn't get me, spend time with me, or nothing, and that was the reason why my grandmother took me in. One of them said, "You know, Dear and the granddaddy adopted her now." At that time, I didn't know I was adopted. I can't remember exactly how old I was but I do remember being devastated. What did they mean by my mother *not* taking me?

I went to school and asked one of the sisters what the word "adopted" meant. She explained to me, "It's when a judge gives somebody else permission to take a child in and take care of them." Then I asked my daddy about it and he broke everything down for me. My daddy and I always had great talks. I would say, "Now daddy, don't lie to me because you know you don't suppose to lie." And he would laugh and always tell me the truth about whatever I asked: what he did to get in prison, life, school, piano lessons, people, and everything. Regarding my mother, he told me he wanted me to have a certain lifestyle that Dear could provide. Besides, he explained, my mom had voluntarily signed my custody papers over to Dear and granddaddy.

Finding out I was adopted really changed my life because, from that point on, I constantly questioned what was so wrong about me that she had given me up, even though she went on to have and keep another child four years younger than me. I battled those questions for years and, as time went on and the older I got, the yearning for my mama grew. I even started getting mad at Dear, the person who loved me with all her heart and soul, because she now completely disallowed that one cousin from seeing me and I thought she was keeping me away from my mama.

One day, one of my mom's sisters came to visit from California and wanted to take me for a while. Dear told her I couldn't go—that was a first because she would usually let me go with her when she came a few hours. I heard my auntie asking why I couldn't go and Dear told her, "Because you're gonna take her around her mamma."

My aunt said, "And if I am, I don't see why that's a problem. It's her mama. You just being low down."

I was listening, secretly agreeing with her.

But Dear said, "I'm not being low down." She had the most soft and pleasant voice. "I said no because I ain't never told her mama that she can't see her or get her. *She* the one who don't. She don't call or nothing."

And it was true. Once I thought about it, I barely ever got a call to say happy birthday or a merry Christmas from my mom. Still, I resented Dear—it wasn't until years later that I understood why she didn't let me go that day. At the time, I was furious at Dear and even got mad at my daddy because he wasn't here with me to make thing right like he always did. I got so mad at the entire world. I felt like no one could talk to me or understand what I was going through. I started closing myself off in my room and became depressed, which neither I nor Dear knew how to deal with. I also began openly hating my cousin who lived with us because she was always picking with me and making my life hell—we fought and argued every day. I realized that you don't have to do nothing to somebody; they can hate you because you exist in the world and they know there's something special about you. I would often say, "I hate her."

Dear would say, "You don't hate nobody. You just kill them with kindness."

Dear really tried. I used to be so sad and she would always ask me what was wrong or if I wanted talk and then say that she would do anything to make things better. Still, there were a lot of issues going on that I couldn't talk to anyone about.

At age fifteen, I became pregnant with my first son and, even though she told me she would beat me down if I ever got pregnant early, Dear was the only person in my corner when word got out. She told me, "I'm here. I'm going to take care of you and that baby. Whatever daycare or school you want him to go to, I don't care how much it costs. All I want you to do is finish school." I promised her that. I had my son on October 17. I was sixteen and, when we came home from the hospital and settled in, Dear said she was going downstairs to make herself a cheese toast. That was when the phone rang for her, but she didn't answer. My little cousin ran downstairs to give her the phone, and then we heard a scream. Something was wrong with Dear.

We ran downstairs. Her face was turned to the left, and she had thrown up on herself. The cheese toast was still hot. She kept looking at me and trying to tell me something but I stopped her from talking or moving. The ambulance came and took her to the hospital. They wouldn't let me go because of the baby, so my aunt rode on. My mean cousin left when her friend came to pick her up but, before she left, she told me it was all my fault. I cried so bad that I threw up. I believed her. I kept hollering, "God, I'm sorry. Please, I love her so much and wouldn't ever want anything to happen to her or would do nothing to hurt her." My baby was crying.

Eventually, my uncle Jolly called and told me to stop crying and to take care of that baby. I kept screaming to him, "I'm sorry," and he told me it wasn't my fault. My grandmother had had heart problems for years and she had already undergone many surgeries.

When my cousin came back from the hospital, she came straight into my room and said, "You need to get you some clothes because you not about to stay here." I asked where I would go. She said, "Call your mama and see if you can go there." I hadn't ever been to my mama's house so I didn't want to go there. Still, my cousin demanded that I leave, so I called my mother, who agreed that my son and I could come stay with her for a few days. I packed accordingly. I thought I would eventually come home, but I ended up being thrown to the streets with nothing but clothes for a few days.

On November 17, the day my son turned a month old, Dear passed away. That's when my life took a turn for the worst. I went into a severe depression while living with my uncle because my mother wouldn't take me anymore and my cousin wouldn't let me come get any of my stuff. She took everything from me, my clothes, shoes, computer, piano, stereo, my son's stuff, accounts Dear had for me since I was a baby—it was like an upside-down Cinderella story. Here I was, sixteen with a baby and no money.

Most teenagers would not have made it, but I wasn't going to be sucked into the statistics of a black, teenage mom in poverty. I wanted to fulfill my promise to Dear about finishing school and to take care of my child. I made it my business to make Dear proud. I took care of my little family by all means necessary, even though they wouldn't let me back in school without a guardian. The devil was still not going to stop me: I got my GED, worked multiple jobs, and eventually got a car. I couldn't yet get an apartment so I stayed with my uncle who provided me with a roof over my head—that was it. Still, I was going to make it and be everything.

After twenty years of hard work, I fought against all odds and the naysayers and have earned everything I ever wanted. I am living my dreams, the life my grandmother desired for me because she believed in me. As a child, I always had dreams of owning a business (that was the budding entrepreneur in me). I used to say that I was going to own a McDonalds, have a big house with a maid and butler, and drive a red corvette.

Now, I may not own a McDonalds, but today, I own two successful businesses with my wonderful husband, Courtney Mays, who loves me, and I am connected to other successful entrepreneurs. We are also blessed with four children, Damonte, DeAnthony, Quianna, and Jala, as well as two stepchildren, Courtariyah and Corniyah, and two grandkids, Rashad and Jace. All the bad are now just memories.

My life has had its ups and downs from depression, attempting suicide, and abuse to molestation, homelessness, loneliness, and losses. But there was a Higher Power Who kept me though the turmoil, and those exact challenges made me into the woman I am today, a woman with a purpose. I've had a lot of comebacks but having to comeback as a teenager made me the beast that cannot be stopped.

So, anybody out there who think it's too hard—I'm here to tell you that you can make it! Stay strong and find a way of no way, even if you have to do it all by yourself. You can win against all odds.

THE WAITING ROOM

Victoria Necole

It was September. So much had already taken place and I was going down what seemed to be another downward spiral of no return. How did I allow myself to get to this place? How could I look my child in the face every day and say, "I love you" when I abandoned another child of God? How could I be so selfish, pathetic, and downright disgusted with myself? Those where the thoughts that ran through my mind when I heard the vacuum sucking out what would have been my second-born.

Yes, it is me: the girl who posts photos of her daughter on Facebook and talks about her being "the light of my life" and "I would do anything for her." But still, there I lay on the clinical bed to receive an abortion. Yes, it is me who said that I would never get an abortion because, when I sleep with someone, I know the outcomes of what can happen from STDs, HIV/AIDS, and an unplanned pregnancy.

So how did I get to this place? Let's rewind to October 2015.

For as long as I can remember, I have been a church girl and I love God. I love going to church and participating in some form of ministry. I knew from a very early age that there was something greater inside of me but, just like most, I didn't want to hear what God had to say and what He had called for me to do. The world, as many of us know, is a lot more appealing than living a saved and sin-free life.

In October 2015, after several life-altering events, I decided to entertain the thought of starting my own organization and working with the youth and adult women who have been affected by domestic violence, especially molestation or rape. So, I held my first meeting. I thought that everyone would root for me, stand in my corner, and tell me, "Victoria, I am so proud of you. I knew you had greater in you!" I wish that had been the case. I won't go so far as to say that no one was cheering me on, but the ones who had seen me go through so much weren't there. The ones I thought would be proud of me and come out and support me were the ones who talked about me the most, saying things behind my back like "Who told her that she could do this?" "She isn't anointed enough to do this?" "Why?"

Sometimes, people who say they love you will be the first ones to run out on you when you try and do better for yourself. They tell you that they are cheering for you but are secretly plotting to take you down. That was how I felt when I decided to take a leap of faith and run with the vision God had given me for my non-profit organization, The Confessions of a Lady (COL). Needless to say, the journey to building my organization was not an easy one.

Just as I birthed COL, I fell into a deep state of depression. Everything that I thought I had overcome rose back up inside of me and, after being rejected by people around me, I turned from church and went back into the world and did what I wanted to do. Popping pills, becoming sexually active, anything to deal with the rejection. But with every action, there's a consequence.

Between 2015-2016, I lost not one apartment but two, got my car repossessed not once but twice. Everything that I was trying to hold on to fell apart and, no matter how I tried to keep it together on the inside, it wasn't coming together on the outside. In March 2016, I met a guy who, if I had been in a healthy state of mind, would have never looked at twice. There wasn't anything wrong with him besides the fact that he had multiple children by different women who had bitter attitudes. What should've stayed a working relationship quickly grew into something more.

In July 2016, I became pregnant. I knew right after the act, but he was sure everything would be fine. Two weeks later, the test proved me right. To my disbelief, I wasn't upset or disgusted, and didn't feel my life was going to end. That night, I called him and went to his house to tell him that I was pregnant. His reply crushed me. After telling me multiple times that he didn't believe in abortions, he told me now that, if I didn't want to have the baby, I didn't have to. Seeing that I was fighting back tears, he turned around again and told me that I could have the baby. It was in that moment that I knew that having a child with this man would put me back in a place that I had been fighting eight-and-a-half years to come out of.

In September 2016, I had my abortion. It was the most terrifying day of my life. I sat in the room with four other women, waiting on my medication to kick in for me to have life sucked out of me. As I lay on that table and the vacuum entered my body, all I could do was cry. Up until this day, I had been calm. Having the talk with the guy about the abortion didn't bother me at all. But, with my feet pressed firmly in the footrest and my butt hanging off the table, with the cold lubricant entering my body, with every twist and turn of the suction, I shed a tear. What was only ten minutes felt like a lifetime.

The doctor looked up at me and told me it was over and that I could get dressed. When the nursed handed me a towel to wipe off the tears in my eyes, I asked her, "Is this the part that people start to cry?" She nodded and told me to take my time. I could leave out and go to the waiting room when I was ready. Once I came out, my ex-would-have-been-baby-daddy sat there and asked why I was crying. Even as I balanced a ton of emotions—guilt, shame, embarrassment—rage trumped them all. How in the world could he ask me why I was crying? What did he think took place in there? I killed a life and I now regretted it. I didn't say anything. I stared at him and he turned his head.

Although I was shameful and disgusted with myself, I knew then that it was the best decision that I could have made for myself. This man wasn't someone I wanted to be connected to for the rest of my life. With him being this insensitive, one of us would have ended up being hurt if I had stayed with him. A child would have made matters that much worse. I regret ever putting myself in a place that led me to the abortion clinic and taking the life of a sibling that I knew my daughter wanted so bad.

I was in and out of sleep on the entire way back to Birmingham as he drove my car. Once we got back, he asked if I wanted him to come over. Half asleep, I cut my eyes at him, not truly understanding why he was asking me this when we had already discussed that he should stay to make sure I was okay through the night. Instead of getting angry, I told him, "No." I felt that, if he had to ask me, then he really didn't want to stay, so we decided to drop him off first so that I could drive myself home. When we pulled up to his apartment, he nudged me to wake up. I was reclined in the passenger seat and told him to hold on for a second for me to gather myself, but I fell back asleep.

When I woke up, he was nowhere to be found. I climbed over to the driver's seat as tears filled my eyes, stomach in knots, palms sweaty. I began to pray to God to cover me as I drove myself twenty minutes across town. I could barely see and I wanted to run my car off the ledge so many times. How, as a mother, could I have killed another life?

Halfway home, I realized that I hadn't eaten. As I pulled into the drive-thru to order food, I began to fall asleep again. I had to pull into a parking space to gather myself. Because I knew that I would not want to leave the house once I got in, I decided to drive to the pharmacy to fill my prescription before I got home. I told the clerk that I would wait on my medication. I was familiar with her since I was a frequent visitor for my daughter's medication. She asked me if I was okay. I instantly broke down and began to cry. All I could think about was whether or not she knew what I had done. Was she judging me? I was replaying the memories in my head and hearing the sound of the vacuum. Guilt was starting to consume me.

I finally made it home, got undressed, took two pills, and got in the bed. I cried into the bread of my sandwich and immediately felt like throwing up. For three nights straight, I had nightmares. First, I dreamt that I was in the local market and, passing a mirror, I saw a dead baby still attached to me with the umbilical cord. I woke up with my sheets wet with sweat. It took me forever to fall back asleep, afraid that, once my eyes closed, I would see the baby there and it would ask me why I didn't want them. The second nightmare, I dreamt that I was sitting at church and heard a baby cry. I looked to my left and there was dead baby stamped with a note, asking, "Why did you kill me?" The third time, I woke up from a dream in another dream with a dead baby. This last night, I woke up and screamed. I asked to please stop making me re-live the pain over and over again. I promised God that, if He took the dreams away, then I would go back to church. That I was sorry, and it wouldn't happen again. The dreams ended but the guilt stayed around constantly for three more months.

Now that it has been a year since the abortion, I can honestly say that it was still the best decision for my life and where God took me. I sometimes reflect on how my life would've been had I gone through with the pregnancy. On one hand, I would've had a wonderful bundle of joy who I would've loved and adored so much as a true blessing from above. On the other hand, how would I have ever taken care of that baby with so little support? Who would I have turned to with no father actively in the house or with family in the same city? Daycare? Formula? What if the baby had gotten sick? Would I have had enough time to take off work to care for the baby?

It took time to heal and to truly accept that God has forgiven me and that I now needed to forgive myself. God told me that if He did it once, He would do it again: in due time, I would have another child with the right helpmate and it won't be a struggle to raise my children. All the sacrifices I had to pay are for me to live the life of abundance. So, today, whenever I need to achieve something, I write out a plan, actively work my plan, revise my plan when necessary, and, when I can't see my next move, I wait for His instructions.

I encourage you to do the same. We face many life-changing decisions each day. You may be a woman who is currently working for a company you love but you've become impatient about a promotion, even though God has told you that you will have a promotion in due time if you are just faithful to your current positions. Or maybe you are a business owner who is still working a full-time job and raising a daughter on your own, but God has told you that you can be your own boss full-time with more flexibility to spend time with your children. Maybe you're in a relationship with someone and God told you to stay, but family and friends are telling you that you can do better and to leave. Whatever it is that you're currently doing that aligns with your purpose, you must work through the pain and cut out the thoughts and worries of everyone else.

You know there's more inside you. This is not the time for you to give up. It's the perfect time for you to work. You're a fighter and giving up isn't an option. God said that, if we are faithful over few, He would make us rulers over many. What we fail to realize is that there is a process and we must be willing to go through the good, the bad, and the ugly to reach the true vision and goal that God has for our lives.

The waiting room experience was one of the most traumatic experiences of my life, but I know that God had to allow me to go through this process in order for me to understand my worth and to get back on track. When you know that you're destined for greater, you have to choose to wait on the Lord and He will renew your strength. You will mount up like an eagle. You will soar and never faint. If you just wait on Him, God will direct your path and give you the strength to win against all odds.

BREAKING CYCLES
More Than A Statistic

Mesia Rena

"The choice is yours Meeshi, never let anyone tell you what you cannot do or become."

Those were the encouraging words my grandfather said to me when I was six-years-old. They will forever be with me. Just a few weeks into kindergarten, I was told to write down my name and age for an assignment. At the time, I was six-years-old, so I wrote my name and my age. My classmate next to me saw my age and told me that it was wrong. He told me to put five. We got into a big argument about it all day, and my classmate called me stupid for not knowing my own age. Little did we know that my birthday was in October but school had started in August. I had to wait a whole year before I could start school, which meant that yes, I was five when I started school but that October I had turned six. Still, my peers were young: they didn't care *why* I was six in kindergarten.

That was my first time being called a name and it made me feel sad. When my grandfather asked me how school was going for me, I told him about my classmate calling me stupid because he thought my age was wrong. That was the first time my grandfather gave me those encouraging words. I didn't understand their true meaning until I got older.

My grandmother told me that, when I was born, the doctor who delivered me said of me, "No worries, just another black girl who will be just like her mother and grandmother—pregnant at fifteen years old, living in a low-income housing community, on government assistance, a high school drop-out, in a fatherless home. We win again." From the day I entered this world, I was already labeled and stereotyped as another statistic. I entered the world fighting for my life, not knowing that the greatest battles were still awaiting me, in my fight to find myself.

Since my mother was young and still in high school when she had me, my grandmother stepped up to the plate to help raise me. From the time I started grade school, my grandmother constantly reminded me how important it was to make good grades. "Don't be like me," she'd say. "Be better than me. Go to school every day, be on your best behavior, and bring home good grades. If you do that, you can go to college."

That was a conversation she and I would have every morning as she got me ready for school. To make sure I was focused in school, my grandmother came up with a reward system. If I brought home all As, I would get five dollars and a special treat; if it was A's and B's, I would just get a special treat. Those rewards were heaven for a kid! So, of course, I made sure my grades were always A's and no B's—I loved my sweets. Little did I know that the simple reward system my grandmother put in place for me would be a major key in my life down the road.

I never understood why the idea of going to college was so important in my family. I was still trying to figure out what I wanted to be when I grew up. I can recall being asked, "Mesia, what do you want to be when you grow up?" My response would always be, "Rich." To which they would respond, "Okay, so what will you be doing to become rich?" I never could answer that question in detail. All I knew was that I wanted to make enough money to buy my grandmother a mansion with her own maid and chef.

The only person I knew that went to college was my mom. She went to junior college but dropped out because she was pregnant with my brother and never went back to finish. As I got older, I continued to excel in school and my grandmother still had her rewards system in place, of course, with a higher payout. At times, I used to feel like so much pressure was on me to not be like my mom or grandmother that I was overwhelmed during my first two years of high school. Everyone told me, "Wow, you are so smart like your mom! We just hope you don't get pregnant like she did." I became unsure of why I wanted to go to college in the first place—was it just to please my family and not disappoint them?

At the age of sixteen, my life took a drastic turn. My grandmother, the woman who motivated and inspired me, died. My first experience of heartbreak. I was mad at the world and at my grandmother for leaving me at a time in my life when I was still trying to figure myself out. I was left alone. My relationship with my mother was totally different from the one I had with my grandmother. Yes, she was my biological mother but I considered my grandmother my real mother and we were always closer. What was I supposed to do now that she was gone?

I had no other choice but to move in with my mother. My mom had always been active in my life even though I lived with my grandmother full-time. I would visit my mother's house and stay a few months with her on and off but my home was with my grandmother. So here I was, a teenager trying to adjust to new living arrangements and new rules that I didn't agree with, so there was much tension between my mother and me. Those first few months were interesting, to say the least.

I called my grandfather one day and told him that I was going to run away from home if he didn't come get me because I wasn't happy living with my mom. My grandfather made some phone calls and some arrangements. By the time I started senior year, I had my own place. That's right, my own place at seventeen-years-old. My grandfather and mother felt like I was mature enough to be trusted on my own, and they continued to support me financially.

I made it! Graduated from high school in the top ten of my class with a full four-year college scholarship and no kids. Cheers to not being another statistic and stereotype, right? But I didn't feel too excited because I was still unsure about going to college. All I heard was my grandmother's encouraging words to continue making good grades. Because I didn't want to disappoint her or my family, I went off to get my higher education. I had no idea what I wanted to major in because all I ever wanted to be was rich. I struggled for two years to maintain a 2.75 GPA to keep my scholarship. My mind wasn't focused because I didn't feel that college was necessary for me. Furthermore, I writher under the pressure of not becoming another statistic.

At the beginning of my senior year I decided to withdraw from college, and get a full-time job instead. The pay was great, but I hated working for the company. I was still not sure what I wanted to do regarding my career, so I settled with being unhappy and working for someone else. I found out that I was pregnant a few months after dropping out of college, and I cried for a week. I really felt like I failed at breaking this generational cycle. Even though I was twenty-one-years-old, I hadn't accomplished anything: still no clear direction of what I wanted out of life and now I was about to bring another life into this world in the same cycle.

The day I heard my unborn child's heartbeat for the first time was the day I got a wake-up call. I refused to bring another life into this world not knowing what I wanted to become and allow them to become another statistic. I vowed to do whatever made Mesia Rena happy and to no longer put others' feelings before mine—I owed it to my baby to be happy and successful.

But twenty weeks into my pregnancy, I went into early labor and gave birth to a one-pound and eleven-ounce baby boy, who died a few minutes after being born. My heart was torn into pieces in the blink of an eye. A part of me died that day. Four months later, my grandfather died. I lost the only father figure I had for the majority of my life. My world was torn again.

Taking the crushing blows of these two tragedies, my heart became numb, but I didn't want to let the outside world know. I pretended to be strong as usual and continued with my everyday activities. I began to drink, party, and shop excessively for the next few years. I was still working for a company that I hated and my life was at a standstill. On the outside looking in, you would see a twenty-five-year-old girl who was full of life, but on the inside, she was hurt and broken and battling dark clouds every day.

Soon, the alcohol could no longer ease the sadness and the only way to get rid of it was to take my life. So, I fixed a glass of water and prepared to take some pills. All I wanted to do was to make the dark clouds disappear and not come back. Before I could put one pill in my mouth, there was a knock on my door. When I opened the door, a Jehovah's Witness was standing before me. At that moment, God saved me.

The next day, I started seeing a therapist. I broke down about losing my grandmother, grandfather, and child and how I never really grieved or talked about these tragic situations. In my family, talking about our issues didn't solve anything; we just learned to deal with them and move on. But they were wrong. I was wrong.

I was diagnosed with severe depression at the age of twenty-five years old. It was during my therapy sessions that I not only got help for my depression but I also finally found myself. I realized that the generational cycle I was trying so hard to break had already been broken the day I graduated from high school. I didn't fail because I dropped out of college and got pregnant like my mother did. It was broken because I did something my mother and grandmother didn't do—I finished high school without getting pregnant. It was still challenging for me to deal with the loss of my family, but I made up my mind that the pity party was over. I welcomed my new independence. Mesia Rena was born again, ready to do what she loved to do, which is to help others. I no longer held on to things I couldn't control and I released myself of the guilt, pain, and found peace within me.

Eventually, I lost my job, and when I couldn't find a new one, I built my own platform and launched my first business. My first business helped women lose weight in their mid-section area and I styled them in the latest fashions to show off their new look. To see the excitement on all my clients' faces and to get so much positive feedback made me feel so good. For the first time, I was doing something that I loved and was 100 percent happy in. I couldn't believe that the young girl who had all the odds stacked against her from the day she was born and who had faced so many different tests and trials in her life was now playing a major part in others' lives. Plus, she was her own boss! I no longer cared about what society said or thought about a young black girl from the projects. I didn't need a college degree to make my dreams come true. I am a grown woman who made it out without being a product of her environment.

Yes, I've made mistakes, but I am here today to tell my story. I came into this world fighting and I will continue to fight for myself. It's my time to live, and yours too. No matter how high the odds may seem to be stacked against you, don't give up. You can change your reaction to what happens to you. If it doesn't work the first time, keep trying. I still deal with my depression today, but because I now have professional help, I'm able to cope better. The journey will not be easy, but it will be worth it in the end.

To keep me going on this journey we call life, I meditate on Philippians 4:13—"I can do all things through Christ who strengthens me"—every day before I start my daily activities. I have taken the encouraging words and lessons that my grandparents provided me with as a child and now use them to my advantage in my personal and professional lives.

In the words of my late grandfather, "The choice is yours. Never let anyone tell you what you cannot do or become." Cycles can be broken. You can win against all odds.

MY UGLIEST BEAUTIFUL

Terria R. Jones

No one ever thinks that going to church would be anything but uplifting and life-changing. In my case, the life-changing part was true in more ways than one.

The trouble began when I came to love my then-pastor as a father, so much so that I wished he was my biological father. Up until then, I thought I didn't need a father because I had my mother. But my pastor's wife had different plans. I don't know if it was the way I ran to him or lit up when he came in the room that changed the way she saw me. Whatever the case, my sisters and I went from being the daughters of good and faithful members to sluts and whores who wanted her husband. This never changed my love for God, but it did change my love for those who called Him their Father, especially those in leadership. The accusations challenged my view of spiritual leaders and even changed the way I viewed myself.

My grandfather, who lived with us, would come down to our room at night and, with a grin on his face, and at eye level he would place his hand on my shoulder. It would be years later before *it* would all come out. However, I never felt right about those nights and, one day while alone with my mom, I simply said, "Let's move and leave granddaddy." I can't remember how she responded, but I was so terrified that I quickly said, "Never mind." I regret ever saying those two little words because they changed my life forever.

This encounter fed into what would soon become my innate distrust for men. I also dealt with men in my life who I trusted and were supposed to protect me, only for them to abuse me in one way or the other. The mental, verbal, and psychological stress and torment for me was a reminder of my past. One thing for sure—I made up my mind that if I ever had kids, especially girls, I would never let them be around men without my presence. Off top, I was always taught to get a man who would provide me whatever I needed, that meant he would give something to me and I would give something to him. That was why it was hard for me to tell people I loved them even if I genuinely did. In my career, I worked with children and felt as if they were all mine, but I didn't know how to express love to them. Therefore, I didn't feel that I was worthy to hold people's children.

That all changed when I met my husband, the first man who I felt I could release my all to. I got married to the man I prayed for; in fact, I wrote God a five-page letter of the type of man I wanted, and God out did Himself in Eric Jones. He showed me how to love and what it means to love. In the beginning, I was afraid of his love and thought that there had to be a catch. But there wasn't. He loved this girl and all the baggage that came with her. Eric is my priest, prophet, protector, and provider. He has taken me from a place of insecurity and uncertainty to assurance and determination. God shows me His love through my husband. Eric is the man who loves hard and loves me, and I needed that.

When I first met my husband, I was eighteen and he was twenty-one. My mom was strict. I wasn't allowed to date so, for the most part, I didn't. So, when I met Eric, I had to sneak…and I was not good at it. Eric would bring me vases of flowers with little cards filled with words of endearment that I still have. But soon, that secret interaction came to an end. I told my mom about him and she made me stop seeing him. It would be three years later that I would reconnect with him.

My uncle was ministering at our now church and Eric recognized him. He asked my uncle to give me his number. I was surprised. I called him that same night and we reconnected. We discovered later that his aunt lived in the same apartment complex I stayed in and we'd never ran into each other. It was all a part of God's master plan.

I wanted Eric to be my boyfriend but, even after becoming a young adult, my mother was against it. She relied on our pastor to make a lot of the decisions that affected us. Still,

I would see Eric when they went out of town, and each time they returned, I told him that I wouldn't be able to see him anymore. I put him through the ringer but he never left and he continued to pursue me.

We would go to his home, the park, a restaurant, anywhere but my apartment. I remember going to his home once and falling asleep. When I woke up, he was there next to me with his hand on my back. That feeling…that feeling I still feel today. I felt security and safety. I knew nothing could hurt me as long as he was there. It was some of the best sleep I have had to date. But I also felt the need to tell him to run and never look back because I was damaged and didn't want him to have to go through all of drama and baggage I came with.

You see, my baggage wasn't conventional: it was of the "holy" kind. Growing up, I was heavily involved in ministry. If I wasn't at work, I was at the church. It was the reason I lived where I did, left school, didn't talk to some family members and friends, and missed out on tons of activities. But it was also the place where I found God; the place where I found out who I was, built relationships, grew—it was My Ugliest Beautiful. But there was still one person holding us back: my pastor. I even left college my sophomore year because I was told by my pastor that we needed to work for the common good of the people and come together on one accord. So, my mom moved out of her three-story house to a two-bedroom apartment, and then eventually into a one-bedroom apartment. Yes, I was dealing with some things.

So, when Eric came into my life, he gave me pure honest love with no strings attached—he just wanted me. I made up in my mind that I wasn't going to keep sneaking around. I was an adult who worked and had an apartment with her sister. You would think I was independent and not under the complete rules of my mother and my pastor. However, they managed those apartments and had keys to our unit. They'd come in and out as they pleased and I had no say. It was really something else, especially with my hindsight being 20/20 vision on the situation.

Eric and I truly had to fight to be together and so we did. He asked me to marry him, not knowing all that he would come to find out. When he met my mom, she told him that I worked in ministry and that I would have to come to the church first before home when I got off work. She encouraged him to learn what I did in ministry and why. And in the most respectful way, he said "No, I will not." He told my mom that, contrary to what she believed, he was not attracted to my breasts or behind—it was the God in me. This took my heart. He stood up for me and what he believed in. He was, even in that moment, taking care of me. He left that encounter with my mom with a new understanding of what it was going to be like to be with me. Still, he stayed.

My mom and pastor's wife started to help plan the wedding, but when conflicts arose, that stopped. My mom ended up not attending her firstborn's wedding. But Eric and I grew, and we became T.E.A.M (those are our first initials, as well as those of our children).

Still, for the first year or two of our marriage, I was depressed. Everything I had gone through was weighing on me. One day, after losing my job, I spent several days in bed. My husband called our new pastor and held the phone to my ear. He asked me what was wrong and said these words: "We don't want anything from you but to love you!" Those words...thirteen years later, I still remember. Those were the words that led to my healing.

What I learned was that, in life, things happen to you and to your family. Still, God is there. He was there through the late-night creep sessions my grandfather would have, through being called a slut, and through depression. He was there when I met my husband, when my now pastor spoke words of life, when I had my two amazing daughters, and when I decided that I was His and that nothing less than the best was good enough for me. I decided to truly take charge of my life.

I'm sure we have all had times in our lives that we wish we could change or people we wish we would've never crossed our paths with. My Ugliest Beautiful is all about those moments in my life that were ugly and appeared to change my life for the worst; but in fact, they shaped me into the woman I am today. I've learned and I am still learning to love without conditions just like my husband. It is so pure, so real, and so honest. His love has caused me to look at myself and find all that is awesome, kind, sincere, daring, and bold, while also exposing the anger, resentment, frustration, and hate I held on to. He continues to give me butterflies even after thirteen years, and helps me be a better wife, mother, friend, and servant.

If you haven't already, I want you to stop and say to yourself, "I can and I will because You can and You will." You have to know that God wants only the best for you. If you are willing to trust Him, you can live again. I learned to trust men again and know that they don't all just want your goodies or have the wrong motives. Some of them just want to love you and are attracted to the God in you and I thank my husband for helping me see that.

Where I once felt unattractive, I am now the makeup artist. Where I once felt like my voice didn't have any authority, I am now using my voice for my ministry announcements. Where I once felt unworthy, my husband and I now have a mentor program for young ladies and men. I've learned to use my ugly to help others become beautiful. The very things that were meant to destroy my ability to love, I'm now using to help others find their most phenomenal self, inside and out. I've learned to conquer what could have destroyed me. I had every reason to never believe in another man, but now God has sent me one man to love me and change my perception of men forever. No matter what you're facing, God has something or someone to help you be made whole. You can truly win against all odds.

THE ART OF PARTNERSHIP

Starnisha Washington

Webster's dictionary defines partnership as "the state or condition of being a partner; participation; association; joint interest." Joint interest is a powerful set of words! It means that two people have something to gain and lose from the situation. Partnerships are developed, not only in business but in almost every area of our everyday lives. Partnerships can be created between you and your spouse, you and your job, you and your friends, and even your kids!

Who am I? I am the average, everyday woman just like you. I am a wife who loves her husband and a mom who lives for her kids. I enjoy hanging with friends on lazy Saturdays and participating in fellowship at church on Sundays. I am the girl you see in the supermarket or run into at the Little League games. I am a woman with dreams and goals just like you. I understand that success is a choice, and I choose success. But what no one told me was that success comes at a price that costs money, time, friends, family, and plenty of tears. It's a road that has peaks and valleys and a lot of pitfalls along the way. Still, it is a road worth staying on course.

Starting out as a young mom of two by the age of seventeen, I was definitely a statistic. No goals or real plans for the future, I was just living life day by day. Playing house was the thing to do and, boy, was I doing it! I was chasing my dreams of living a certain type of lifestyle through someone else. It never occurred to me that, inside of myself, I was holding the keys to give myself everything I was looking for and more.

Sitting in my little apartment one day as my birthday was approaching, I did my annual self-evaluation. You know, the ones where you are completely blunt and honest with yourself. I wrote down all of the pros and cons of my life. People, places, and things that held value and those that did not. If you can be real with yourself—I mean *really* real—this can be a major eye-opener. Of course, I didn't like what I read and, at that moment, I woke up! I vowed to change. It was time for a life plan.

It is only when we can truly be honest with ourselves that we can bring about real change. Sometimes, we allow our circumstances to define us and build our characters around that. But your circumstances don't define you. As I searched for something new, I decided to tackle the giant of entrepreneurship. I always knew I had the ability to run a business, but ability without vision is nothing at all. If you just perform the things you're good at, you will be surprised what you can create from there.

Along came my very first business. I opened a retail store and rocked it. My confidence went through the roof and so did my bank account. To see my life change also changed who I was. I was no longer that girl without plans or goals. I was now the girl whose future was bright. I knew that the talent, skills, and knowledge I learned along the way were invaluable (it also didn't hurt that my mom held a master's degree in business). As the years went by, I ran my business successfully and mastered the craft of entrepreneurship. Making sure that I learned the ends and outs was extremely important to me. I also wanted to make sure that, one day, I could teach someone else how to make their dreams come true like I did.

As I dabbled in the retail industry for a few years, I was excited when a new opportunity came along. I knew my worth and thought that my resume spoke volumes so I could tackle any new venture effortlessly. Boy, did I underestimate what I was getting myself into! Just when you think you have formed a plan for your future, life kicks you in the gut and takes you ten steps in the opposite direction. But holding on to your determination is key!

The new business venture required me to enter into a partnership since another individual and I were purchasing a franchise. When I say franchise, I mean a lucrative franchise that had the capability of catapulting my business goals into the stratosphere.

Basing my decision off my skills, ambition, and business knowledge was my very first mistake. What about my partner's skills, ambition, and knowledge? In business, it is extremely important that we always protect ourselves properly. You must not only look at how you will benefit from the venture but also the entire structure of the business.

When you are purchasing a franchise, you are essentially purchasing someone else's business model (your partner's, to be exact). You will be limited as to what part of your vision you can implement into the business. Now, don't get me wrong: there are some franchises out there and partnerships that work out great. It's just that everything, and I do mean *everything*, needs to be discussed upfront.

Months into the partnership/franchise venture, the business became extremely successful and business-wise, we were doing great! But partnership-wise, I quickly realized that I had gotten a landmine instead of a goldmine. It was my knowledge, ability, and skill that built the business, not those of my partner. Then, overnight, I found myself in the fight of my life. My business partner was attempting to take the business from me! Thankfully, I protected myself with a detailed partnership agreement. Pro tip: don't go into business with anyone (there are no exceptions to the word *anyone*) without a detailed partnership agreement. Details are important.

The problem was not the paperwork; the issue was that we physically had to work together daily and no longer wanted to be in partnership together. Imagine finding yourself in a situation where you are extremely unhappy and the only way out is to accept defeat. If you don't, the cost you pay is your sanity. When things go wrong, we sometimes stay in a place that God is ready to move us from because we don't want to accept defeat.

It was certainly a struggle for me. Remember now, I chose success so to accept defeat was just out of the question! However, holding on was becoming too expensive and I quickly began to pay the price. My partner and I fought daily over how to separate the business without either of us losing. The thing about being in a bad relationship is that, the longer you stay, the worse things get. You may end up fussing and arguing daily—this now costs you your character. If you are in a bad domestic relationship and the thought of your partner being home when you get there makes you cringe, you are now paying with your peace. I won't even mention how much of your time it costs you. We must be extremely careful what type of partnerships we get into because the cost you pay may not be worth it.

My choice to surrender and wave the white flag was a hard one to make. Even though the decision was hard, I wanted my peace, my sanity, my character, my time…I wanted everything back! I wanted to be normal again. I walked away from a business I was excited about, one I had built and created from the ground up, and left everything with someone who didn't deserve it.

Now, regardless of whatever type of partnership you are dealing with, if you ever have to dissolve that partnership, make sure you do it right. When you are in the moving-on process, it is imperative that you are intentional about leaving the resentment behind and looking towards the future. As for me, I turned my back on the entire situation and planned to allow the courts to handle it for me. When I say I turned my back, I mean I didn't look back at all. I took my life back vigorously. I read daily affirmations and reminded myself that life is full of hills and valleys. I began to work on loving and taking care of myself. I reminded myself that the same skills and ability that I had going in the door, I still had. The difference was that, now, I had expanded my knowledge even more. Now, I knew another avenue of business I didn't know before. My knowledge was my power! Slowly but surely, my emotional account as I call it, began to fill back up

The following are the three key facts to establishing a successful partnership, whether it be business or otherwise:

1. **Always protect yourself.** Starting a new venture can be exciting and fun. But what happens when the fun wears off? What happens when you are not as excited going out as you were going in? I don't care if you are going into business with your mother—protect yourself with a

solid-legally binding partnership agreement. It's not personal, it's just business. Money tends to change people.

2. **Learn your partner.** When you start a new job, you are always placed on a ninety-day probation. This is a "getting to know you" phase. Your boss is looking to see what kind of work ethic you have and if you are a good fit for the company.

Why don't we do the same in life? If you are entering a new relationship, learn your partner. Get to know their friends and family, their likes and dislikes, their spiritual walk. Ask questions, do your homework. Don't just fall for a few nice gifts and kind words. People can be who you want them to be when you don't know the real them.

As far as business goes, these are the days of technology. Plain and simple: Google your partner! See what comes up when you Google their name, their spouse's name, their momma's name, the people closest to them. A successful business means that plenty of money will be involved and you need to know what you're dealing with. Also, make sure you run extensive background checks. Even if you are going into business with your high school friend and you think you know everything about them, nobody really knows everything about anybody. A good background check can cost a few dollars but it's better to pay now than later.

3. **Choose your partner objectively.** The only reason you should even consider a partnership of any kind is because you wish to align yourself with like-minded people with similar goals. Make sure that, when choosing a partner, they possess skills that will be an asset to the team. I may be great at marketing and merchandising and you may be great at bookkeeping and sales. Your strengths must complement my weaknesses and vice versa.

   Never pick your partner based on finances alone. Opening a new business can be expensive and quite a risk—trust me, I understand that two bank accounts are definitely better than one. Finances, however, are not enough for a strong partnership. You need finance *and* skill. There's nothing like a little sweat equity! Everyone involved must bring something to the table in addition to finances. I'm ying, you're yang, and together, we are powerful.

In life, we go through things that may appear as if they are designed to take us out. But it is not about how well you accept the hardship or defeat but how well you bounce back. My momma always told me that we had BBA—Bounce Back Ability—and, after my ordeal, I was determined that my comeback was going to be greater than ever before.

Always understand that *you* are the "it" factor! It is not about your circumstances or situation. I'll say this again: knowledge is power. Take the situation, learn from it, and allow it to push you to grow. I made the decision to start my own company again. Not in the retail field that I was once in, but now in the new lucrative field I had learned about while someone was trying to defeat me. Once I changed my circumstances, I began to see all the blessings that were in disguise. God has a funny way of teaching us at times. Yes, I lost my business, battled depression because of it, and almost lost my mind. At that time, my drive to succeed would not allow me to see the small things. I could only focus on the failure, but failure is needed sometimes! And *I failed* myself—I wanted the opportunity so bad, I was willing to overlook all of the red flags in order to get it.

As women, we tend to do this with new relationships: we overlook all the flaws because we want the end result. But what happens when the end result becomes detrimental to your well-being? Is it really worth it? Now let me ask you another question: how often do you actually pray first and allow God to lead? When I say allow Him to lead, I mean even when the answer He gives is not the one you want to hear. If He says, don't open that business, just don't. If He says, that man is not the man for you, walk away. It's okay to lose in order to win! Once you are out of your pit, you will definitely enjoy the comeback. God gives His toughest battles to His strongest soldiers because He knows you will win with grace.

Through my experiences, I've learned how to avoid the landmines in life. I learned how to accept life's ups and downs and how to do it graciously. I am now able to generate money in a new way on a whole different level. I went from being the franchisee to the franchisor. I learned how to deal with issues and keep my emotional account on full. I went from setback to comeback! And I learned how to win against all odds.

The right partnership can be a goldmine, the wrong can be a landmine...it costs to learn the difference!

BEYOND BROKE AND LOVING WHAT I DO

Nicole Johnson

In 1996, I thought my life was over. I found myself sitting in a federal courthouse with a room full of strangers. We all had one common goal: to ask a bankruptcy judge to wipe away our debts. I kept asking myself, "How did this happen?" I didn't know.

My attorney assured that me everything would be fine. He told me that I would get a new beginning to my financial life. Even though that sounded great, I was crying inside. Sure, I looked calm and collected on the outside, but I was biting my bottom lip and praying the tears away. At the age of twenty-four, I was a single mother, just out of a broken relationship, and in emotional and financial wreck. And to make matters worse, I didn't know what to do to get my life in order. When you know better, you do better. But I didn't know better.

I was broke! Financially broke! Emotionally broke! Bankrupt! But I was not out of the game. Have you ever been in a place in your life where you wanted to do things differently, out of the box, but didn't know how? Did you feel stuck? That was me.

I am the oldest of four girls and my mother ruled with an iron hand. I never understood how she could be so strong yet remain in an abusive relationship with her live-in boyfriend. I was an outspoken young lady. I probably spoke my mind at times when I should've only been seen and not heard. I'd always stood my ground and never back down, even when her boyfriend came for me. He might've won in the end, but the cops would know he'd been in a fight!

That went on for years. My mom would pack us up to go stay with grandma until they made up. I remember days in our apartment where we had to whisper because he was angry with her and, if he was angry, nobody else could be happy. It was an awful existence. To this day, I still struggle with abandonment issues. But that's another story.

A few days after my high school graduation came another round of pack-up-and-leave because he jumped on her again. This time, I stayed with my aunt. I waited a few days before I called my mother. Truthfully, I didn't want her to tell me that "we" were going back home. When I called, my grandma told me my mother had already gone back. I didn't want to go. With tears in my eyes, I told my aunt that I didn't want to go return to that miserable home.

When I called, my mother told me that she didn't want me to come back home either. Things had been better since I was gone. Talk about a gut punch. After a few minutes of tears, my aunt walked me into the bathroom, told me to clean my face, and look in the mirror. It was at that moment she told me that the only person I could ever depend on was the person in the mirror. I needed to get my head in the game and take care of myself. Something inside of me changed that day. I no longer had a mother. It was just me. And at the age of eighteen, how could that be? Legally, yes, I was an adult but I was not ready to take on the world.

In the fall of 1990, I headed off to Illinois State University, not with my head held high but with a sigh of relief. College was my escape! My escape from the bastard who beat me and the mother who failed me. I was free to do what I wanted. I was trusting me…that was a huge mistake! While my mother was teaching me what not to do as a mother, she didn't teach me how to be a college student or how to avoid credit card applications that came with a free t-shirt. Furthermore, I soon realized that my head was not in the game for school. I returned home to Chicago after my second semester. I had not found my inner strength. *Yet.*

Let's fast forward a little bit: I was now twenty-two and pregnant. Remember those credit card applications that nobody warned me about? Well, the bills started piling up. Then charge-off letters started showing up. Then collection agency letters! Whoa, maybe I needed to read them? But what bills could I pay with a baby on the way? Oh well, back to tossing them in the garbage. Two years later, I was a single mother, still trying to figure out life for me and now my little girl. And guess what? I was failing. Then, it was 1996 and I was in the federal courthouse, asking a bankruptcy judge to relieve me of my debts. The court approved my bankruptcy petition, but I felt like a failure. I swore that bankruptcy would never be an option for me again.

In 1998, my ex-boyfriend became my husband. I managed our money well and, in 1999, I gave birth to our son. Due to some health issues with our new baby, I quit my job to stay home while my husband worked. Being a stay-at-home mom drove me crazy! So, one day, I walked to the neighborhood Jackson Hewitt tax office and took the class to become a tax preparer. Little did I know that I had just tapped into my entrepreneurial spirit.

By 2001, my ex-boyfriend turned husband was well on his way to becoming my ex-husband. See, this is what happens when you pick for yourself and ignore all the warning signs from God that clearly say, "He is *not* the one." I filed for child support before filing for divorce. I was every bitch under the sun for doing so and that was just the beginning of that fight.

Now, child support was not enough to replace his income and I was just getting back to work. How was I going to make it? I tried direct sales for a telecommunications company then a candle business, and loved the independence that it gave me. I loved being an entrepreneur and now it was time for me to figure out how to make it a successful business. I still had not found my inner strength. *Yet.*

In 2003, after finalizing my divorce and being involved in a house fire (again, another story), guess what? The "B" word was my only option. That's right, I filed bankruptcy, *again.* This time, I did not feel like a failure. This time, I really felt like I was taking this step to become whole in my financial life. Shortly thereafter, I relocated to Georgia then Alabama where I began working for the State of Alabama Child Support Department. Life *seemed* to settle down for me and my kids. But there was something missing. I still hadn't tapped into my inner strength. *Yet.*

In early 2008, I went to a housing seminar to learn about becoming a homeowner. The speaker talked about the ease of the program, how affordable it was, and how quickly one could become a homeowner *if* their finances and budget were in order. I thought, could I leave now? I didn't have a budget and my finances were in disarray. Does that count as "order?"

A few weeks later, I was fussing at my kids about turning off the lights when they were not using them. I asked them if they knew how much it cost to live here. My so, so smart daughter said, "What, like $2 or $300 dollars?" I thought, is she serious? Let me *show her!*

I snatched up my check register and started calling about all the payments to the rental company and utility companies. Before it was over, I had an ah-ha moment. If I could spend this type of money for this apartment, I could have for a house! *That* was the moment that I tapped into my inner strength. That was the moment that I changed my mindset and decided to become a homeowner, as well as fulfill my lifelong dream of going to law school to become an attorney.

I *finally* tapped into my inner strength and she is a beast! I surprised myself! Years ago, a business associate told me that he admired my tenacity. I didn't grasp the depth of what he spoke, but, when I tapped into that inner strength, I understood and felt like all seven wonders of the world. I realized that God had planted a seed in me and it was now my time to walk into my destiny. He made me tenacious. He gave me the determination to endure.

It took a great skill-set to work full-time, go to school three nights a week, raise two children, and still find time to cook, clean, grocery shop, study, eat, and sleep! And in the midst of all of that, I taught myself how to budget so that I could become a homeowner. I pulled my credit reports. I tracked my spending and discovered where my money was actually going. I took a Dave Ramsey class at my church. I began to learn the importance of credit cards and how to use and not to use them. I became a new person. I found my love in finances and my desire to help others learn how to manage their finances. If you could do it, so could they.

In the summer of 2008, I enrolled in Miles Law School. In May 2009, I transferred to the Birmingham School of Law. I left the State of Alabama and began working at the Social Security Administration. This change in jobs delayed my home-buying process but on September 9, 2009 I became a first-time homeowner. The feeling was amazing!

I was so excited to tell other people about the programs that helped me during my process that I began using Facebook to share my newfound information. One day while scrolling through a group I was in, someone asked about the program that I had used. And while I was typing my story, a ton of negative comments were posted about the program. So, I started my own Facebook group to let people know that yes, the program has its flaws but it could become an immense tool if one keeps their mind focused on their goals. I realized then that I could be a voice of reason for people who needed help and were confused about certain processes in homeownership.

My next major accomplishment was that my son, my daughter, and I all graduated with the Class of 2013. He came out of middle school, she came out of high school, and I graduated with my master in public administration in October 2013 *and* my Juris Doctor (law degree) in December 2013.

I shared my testimony for the following reasons:

1. **To give God the glory.** He has brought me a long way and, to this day, He carries me through. My child support, my job, my side hustles are just vessels. He is my provider.

2. **To give those of you who need it some encouragement.** Changing your outlook on your money is a lifestyle and mindset change. Look at your challenge as a pie. How do you eat a pie? One slice at a time!

3. **To remind *you* to celebrate you!**

I am still pressing forward. Today, I have taken my passion for teaching others about financial management, budgeting skills, and homebuyer preparation and turned it into my financial literacy company, B & B Financial Services, where I help clients see their financial future clearly.

This has been an amazing journey despite the rough beginnings and the awful middle parts. I am beyond broke and loving what I do. If you are feeling lost, helpless, and hopeless because you have made some past financial mistakes—don't. Know that you are not alone. You are not the last. But you can make some changes! Although you may be overwhelmed financially, you have the power to change it. You are one decision away from your comeback. You can truly win against all odds.

REACHING OUT TO GIVE A HAND UP

Geonisha Brown

Many times, a story of your survival that inspire others often illuminate realizations in your own self. Despite the fact that I had survived the worst in my life, there was still a part of me that was broken. A part of me that I thought I lost, but in actuality, I was waiting to find who I truly am. This part of me had to break, so that a bigger and better part of me could be built. There is always more to a story than just an enticing cover. It is hard to understand what others go through, simply because we've never experienced their particular struggle or faced adversities filled with unbelievable obstacles.

I, personally, never thought I would be the woman I am today: Strong, Sensible. Smart. Beautiful (both inside and outside). Courageous. God-Fearing. Optimistic. Driven. Determined. Always willing to fight for what I believe in. But there is always more to a story than just an enticing cover. It's often so hard to understand what others go through, simply because we've never experienced their particular struggle or faced adversities filled with unbelievable obstacles. I'm proud that I can look back and say, "I faced that." So, who are you, you ask? My name is Geonisha Brown but most people who know me call me Geo. I am twenty-five years young, but most importantly, I am alive.

September 16, 2012, my life was put on the line to see if it was worth keeping. I was in a horrible car wreck with another car and an eighteen-wheeler tractor-trailer. I was coming down I-459 from Tuscaloosa, heading home to Hueytown. I don't remember anything except the last four days in the hospital after being there for a whole month. According to the police report, I was in the middle lane when the other car and the tractor-trailer were in the right-hand lane. The other driver claims that I attempted to get over in his lane but did not see him in my blind spot. Suddenly, the back end of my car was on the top of his hood.

He claims that he got off the interstate and onto the shoulder, while my car sped up, spun out of control, and ran head first into the concrete barrier in the middle of the lanes. The tractor-trailer driver says that he saw something about to happen with the other car driver, so he decided to switch lanes to get behind me. I was immediately thrown fifty feet out of my car and the front half of my body scrubbed the cement for about another fifty feet before my body came to a stop. The tractor-trailer driver says that with my body now on the interstate, my car did a 360 back into traffic and he barely missed running me over. Instead, he took my car down the interstate, literally crushing it to the point that they had to lift the whole front of the 18-wheeler up to pull its mangled and crushed body from up underneath it. They only identified the scrap metal as my car after my mother brought in paperwork to prove it.

It was bad. Very bad. According to my medical reports, I lost most of the blood in my body. I had a tooth in the front knocked out along with several other chipped teeth, multiple abrasions where my skin was scrubbed down to the white meat, and glass in my hair that had lodged into my scalp. My lungs had collapsed. Mind you, I have asthma and bronchitis so that was just my luck, huh? On top, I also had to have my right foot and part of my leg above the ankle amputated. My foot was split open from in between the big toe and the second toe to above my ankle. The wound, being exposed for too long, quickly became infected and rose up my leg, so my doctor and mother made the executive decision to cut it off.

My family and close church family members later told me how distressed my mother was when she received news of my accident during church service. She was already worried about her baby girl, since I had already texted her hours before to tell her I was on my way home. I truly thank God for such a faith-filled family and church family because they saturated my room with prayer and uplifting gospel CD music. Not to mention that God blessed me with an orthopedic doctor who is a man after His own heart.

I was in a coma for a while. When I finally awoke, my memory was gone for a few days and I had to have a breathing tube placed down my throat because my lungs refused to work on their own. I even remember being unconscious but conscious: it felt like I was in a dark room where I couldn't move or talk or even see but I could hear everything that was going on around me. The one conversation I remember so well is when I overheard the doctor telling my mom that they were contemplating putting a hole in my throat to try and help me breathe but even that might not help me given the condition my lungs were already in.

I think most had no faith in me because of what they've been taught through science and not what God can do despite how things look in man's eyes. I also remember two people coming into my room to check all of my vitals and one person said to the other, "Maybe we should tell her mom to prepare for her funeral arrangements so at least she can be ready." It felt as if no one knew how it felt to be in a situation like that—not being able to control the outcome or even begin to be able to help. It was all up to God. Only He would decide what the outcome would be.

Fast forward some weeks later, the pain in my leg kept me up at night so I barely slept. One night, when the pain was so unbearable, I started watching TV to distract myself. Joyce Meyer was ending and Joel Osteen was beginning his sermon. He said, "Instead of us Christians always going to God for something like He is the bank, why don't we just sincerely thank Him for what He has already done for us? Often, we take from God with the promise of paying Him back or never doing it again that we forget to appreciate Him for the ways He has already made for us. God already knows what we want and need but He just needs to know if we care and love Him, or even appreciate what He does on the regular. Try thanking God right now and watch Him move."

I could not talk because of the breathing tube down my throat but I said silently to myself, "Thank You, God. If You did nothing else, You've saved my life and that is all that matters. I do not care if I never walk again because at least I have my life." After that prayer, I went from being on my deathbed to healthy and able to go home to heal in peace in just four days. *Four days!* My relationship with God comes purely from my experiences with Him and who He has proven Himself to be in my life, not what my family and church instilled in me.

But moving on—it was an adjustment trying to adapt to a life of being physically disabled. Up until then, my right side had been my dominant side; but after losing that ankle, I had to learn how to depend on and trust my left side. For months, I could not sit up without keeling back over, so I had to be under constant supervision. I needed assistance with going to the bathroom and my mother had to bathe me for months until I could do things on my own again. The house we lived in was not accessible for me and my needs, so it was an even bigger and harder adjustment for my mother and brothers to help me do everything. I will be honest—my accident put a strain on our relationship. My younger brothers were tired of having to do everything for me, and my mom was stretched way too thin, trying to work to cover regular bills and expenses in addition to meeting my necessities.

I am a strong believer that an idle mind is the devil's playground because, so many times, the enemy reminded me of what was wrong with me and what I could not do and who I was not anymore. I felt so worthless. So broken. So empty. So ugly. A burden on my family. All they did was complain about having to help me. I even downed a half bottle of pain pills one day, thinking I could just end it all. I just did not want to be here because of the way that the people closest to me made me feel. I was usually a happy person but, this time, my spirit was broken, and I just could not see a light at the end of my tunnel called life. But God said otherwise.

First of all, He blessed me with a my church family who never treated me differently. Then, He made me an inspiration: when people saw me face the giants in my life instead of giving up, it encouraged them to go through and face their own situations as well. It became a domino effect of people meeting me and thinking, "Wow, if she can then so can I."

Of course, it wasn't all happy and uplifting times. I had my moments when I couldn't take it any longer. It took many weeks of crying and praying, but God gave me peace that surpasses all understanding. I am so grateful that He granted my request because my peace in Him is what gave me the strength and energy to go through, even if I did not feel like pushing myself. His peace, mercy, and love are what kept me grounded in wanting to just continue living my life. I didn't know how I was going to make it, but I was assured that every day being alive would be a chance to be and do better than I was and did the day before.

I may be young but I have learned that life is not about what happened or didn't happen to us; instead, it's about who we choose to be above it all. I chose to tell myself that I was going to make it despite what the doctors or the world or the naysayers thought and said about me. It always felt like I was running on thin air until I changed my perspective and realized it was just God holding me even when the world could not give me a foundation to stand on.

Here is how I view life now: let's say, for instance, you are on your way to work and you take your regular route. Suddenly, there is an accident right in front of you. First, this event brings your routine to a halt. Second, you now must come up with a plan to get to work via a different route. This route may take you longer to get to work and you might be late. You may even get lost on the way, but your destination does not change.

No matter what shows up in our path, our destination is still the same. Our obstacles allow us to know what we are made of, to help better ourselves for our next level. How dare you ask God for strength then get mad when He allows pressure to be applied to you? If a situation was meant to take you out, then God wouldn't have let you live to tell the story. Your death is what the devil intends but God is the real decision-maker.

Your death is what the devil intends, but God is the real decision-maker. He will work it out for your good. You can win against all odds. Where does your faith really lie?

GET OUT OF YOUR OWN WAY

My Story of Infertility and How I Almost Talked Myself Out of The Promises of Yah

....

Stacey Yvonne

For as long as I can remember, I've always wanted to become a mother. As a young girl, I always wanted a large family because I came from a very, very small family. I have no siblings, and my mother lived in Atlanta, Georgia most of my childhood years, while my grandmother and I lived in Birmingham, Alabama. I was very much alone during my childhood, my desire to mother my own family was great.

During my teenage years, I tried to get pregnant. Although I didn't have many sexual partners, I was very promiscuous. I did a lot of things that I'm not proud of. At nineteen, I got married. Though we never used contraception, for the first six years of that union, I did not conceive. I was depressed. There were so many people around me, married and unmarried, getting pregnant; some who I believed didn't deserve to be mothers.

There was a reason I had such a hard time conceiving. I was diagnosed as a teenager with a condition called polycystic ovarian syndrome (PCOS). I never really gave it much consideration in my young adulthood until I started trying to have children. My ex-husband and I went to my OBGYN and had a series of tests ran on us both. Tests showed that he was fine and so was I. There was nothing in the natural that was hindering us from conceiving, but my doctor was so compassionate to my situation that she prescribed me a drug called Clomid to produce multiple eggs during ovulation. He also gave my ex-husband a cream called Androgel to rub on his abdomen to increase testosterone and his sperms mobility. We did that faithfully for about seven months and nothing! I felt so defeated and felt like it was me who couldn't give us hope for children. It was rough for me mentally and I imagine it was for him too, but he never said a word or showed any type of disappointment to me.

Around age twenty-five, I was still having no luck at getting pregnant. I started to focus more on losing weight, not for health reasons but because I wanted to look better. I stopped focusing on getting pregnant: at that point, I began to feel like all the things I'd done in my teenage years—drugs, lying to men about being pregnant when I wasn't, being disobedient and disrespectful to my mother, the list goes on—

was proof that I would be a poor mother and that was why I didn't deserve children.

After I lost my first fifty pounds, I felt great! My cycles started regulating and I felt more energetic and full of life. Then, in April 2007, my period was late. I just happened to mention it in conversation while I was on the phone with my cousin, and she said, "I really believe you should take a pregnancy test." I was skeptical because I really didn't think that was possible anymore and I also didn't want to get my hopes up high. Still, I went and got one pregnancy test and told my mom and ex-husband what I was doing. We all waited for the stick to change…and it was positive! I couldn't believe we did it. No fertility assistance, no medicine, no expectations, nothing. I called my doctor and scheduled my first prenatal appointment for the following week.

Two days later, I started to spot and my doctor called me in. We learned that it wasn't a viable pregnancy and I was miscarrying. They told me there was nothing they could do and sent us home. I was so crushed. My ex-husband took it very well and just said there would be another chance and consoled me as best he could. No less than six weeks later, I was pregnant again. I went to my first prenatal appointment and got to see the baby moving around. I heard the heartbeat. During my next checkup at nine weeks, they did another ultrasound and the baby looked exactly the same. No movement, no heartbeat.

I had to have a procedure called a DNC to remove the dead baby. From that point on, I suffered one tubal pregnancy and two more miscarriages all within a matter of a six to seven-month span. The doctors did a lot of tests to see what was causing these miscarriages and found out that I have a blood-clotting disorder caller Factor V Leiden, which causes no harm to me, but forms blood clots in the placenta. The baby cannot survive in such an environment. I was put on a blood thinner called Heparin, which I had to inject into my abdomen twice a day while pregnant, but it was always too late by the time I found out.

My mom was on the medical staff at her church at the time, and she had a group of people praying for us and our situation. One day, a man (I still don't know who he is) walked up to her and told her that he and his family had been praying for me. He said, "Tell your daughter to get a book called *Supernatural Childbirth* and read it."

I got the book without much expectation and read it. That book showed me that I wasn't alone in the way that I was feeling, taught me how to pray and confess without feeling like a burden or inconvenience to Yah (God), and outlined ways to change my mindset. You see, I was walking in self-sabotage. I thought and believed that I was unworthy, undeserving, unfit, and not good enough to be a mother. I thought Yah had turned His face from me for all the wrong I'd done and I was now reaping a harvest of my own seed. But I soon realized that we serve a forgiving Father and, even though we may have done things and got in our own way, He is merciful. He will not turn His face from you. He did not turn His face from me.

In December of 2007, I found out I was pregnant again and started my Heparin. I also prayed daily (even before I got pregnant, I had started praying and confessing my desires to Yah), taking my meds, and going to work at the Flowers Baking Company where I was required to do a lot of walking, standing and lifting. I lived in shear fear! Although I confessed daily that "I was not given a spirit of fear, but of love, power and of a sound mind," it had not fully manifested (2 Timothy 1:7).

One day while at work, I started to spot again. But this time, I didn't feel any terror. In my mind, I knew my prayers were covering me. My doctor called me in right away (side note: I pray that you find a good medical team who's understanding and compassionate because I was always taken care of no matter how much I called or came in). They checked me via ultrasound and the baby was fine. She put me on bed rest and, for the duration of that pregnancy, I was on bed rest off and on a total of six months.

I gave birth to my first son on August 20th 2008. Since then, I've given birth to three more children and I chose not to do the Heparin injections for the duration of the last two pregnancies. While I do not encourage anyone to go against their doctor's orders, I knew and felt in my heart that the Heparin was not the reason my children made it to this world.

Now that I've told you my story in brief, I want to talk to you and give you encouragement if you've ever experienced anything like this or if you know someone who has.

First of all, you are enough! Whatever you have convinced yourself to believe about you and your situation, throw it out of your mind. It is so very important that you start here. Romans 12:2 reads, "Do not be conformed to this world but be transformed by the renewal of your mind, that by testing you may discern what is the will of Yah (God), what is good and acceptable and perfect." Please erase all negative doubt and self-talk, and forgive yourself for whatever you've done in your past to make you feel unworthy. You are worthy.

Second of all, please do not compare your situation to others. Your journey is not their journey. The path you walk is meant for you and you only. I fully believe that my experience with infertility created a path for me to be compassionate to women and men who experience similar losses and to give them hope through the promises of Yah and what He did for me. When I was recovering from the DNC, my first cousin was also pregnant with her first child. She came to my home where my mother was also living with my then-husband and myself. She showed my mom a video of her baby on the monitor and they watched it on TV while I laid there expelling the remnants of a baby.

That really put me in a place of anger. I went to Yah again and wanted to know why that had happened to me. There are some women who can sneeze, be pregnant, and not even want their children. But I wanted children, was married, employed, thought I was doing it all right, and I still couldn't hold a baby.

Stop here and learn from my mistake: *remove this type of thinking!* That is the devil's way of making you fall into self-pity, and you will talk yourself right on out of the blessing that awaits you. Our timetable is nothing like Yah's. Oh, how I look at life now and I thank Him. He helped me become a mother when I did because my children would not have had the same mother they have now. I wasn't this mature, kind, or self-loving. In fact, I was still dealing with childhood issues: that pain and trauma could have trickled into the way I parented my children and caused another cycle of generational curses.

I know that a waiting woman doesn't want to hear "be patient." But I am telling you, get yourself ready for the blessing. Be patient. Don't see the situation with your natural eye. Yah will make time at the right time. No matter your age or circumstances, your time will come.

Third, I want to strongly encourage you to start praying, confessing, and making your petitions to Yah. Ask for what you want! No matter how small it seems to you, tell Him because He knows your heart anyway. You know how it is to know that someone wants something and you have the means to give it to them *but* you want to see how serious they are, so you wait until they ask. I imagine it's the same for Him. The Bible says in Psalm 55:22 ESV, "Cast your burdens on the Lord, and He will sustain you; He will never permit the righteous to be moved." And 1 Peter 5:7 ESV also says, "Cast all your anxieties on Him, because He cares for you."

Remind Him of His promises to you and show Him how your desires make you feel. He said, "Be fruitful and multiply and fill the earth." He meant you too! Psalm 113:9 says, "He gives the childless woman a family, making her a happy mother. Praise the Lord."

Lastly, get you a strong circle of people to pray for you. I realize all walks and religions are not the same, so whatever your belief is, get a strong circle within to pray with and for you. Infertility is a matter of the heart and mind, so we can get into our emotions sometimes and don't always have the strength to pray. That's where your circle will come in and intervene on your behalf. I had people praying for me that I didn't even know. I say to them, if they ever read this: thank you.

Get ready, mentally, physically, and spiritually. Whether you are waiting for a baby or your big break, it's coming. I pray that my story helps and encourages you. Always remember that, if you don't have a circle, you have me praying on your behalf. Get out of your own way and stand on the Word. It worked for me and it will work for you. You can win against all odds.

THE PALM TREE EFFECT
*Bending in the Midst of the Storm
but Never Breaking*

Crystal M. NeVille

Hawaii, Florida, California, and Cozumel! I would love to visit any of those places and enjoy the year-round warm climate and beautiful scenery, which always includes palm trees. You know those tress that some see in their dreams as they relax on an island or a sandy beach, sitting under an umbrella with a tall glass of ice tea and feeling the breeze blow as if you were in paradise. Palm trees are the symbol of relaxation and stress relief from the day-to-day cares of life.

Now let me introduce you to those same palm trees in another light. Hurricane season: those same beautiful trees that make you think of those old commercials that said *CALGON, TAKE ME AWAY* must now face intense conditions, forced to withstand winds that would blow us over with ease.

However, palm trees were created by God to survive in regions where they flourish. Yes, regions with palm trees are usually the same regions that produce hurricanes.

Hurricane X, Y, or Z comes on land and destroys property, impacts communities for months, and even claims lives. At the same time, these same palm trees won't break: their leaves, roots, and bark work together to bend back and forth even to the point of being horizontal to the ground. The beautiful trees of our vacation dreams are built to last through tumultuous wind and rain.

That's how our God created you and me. Let me take you on a journey through my hurricane to my comeback.

In the sixties and seventies, this little black girl grew up in the community of Norwood in Birmingham, Alabama with my parents, Walter and Mary Jenkins, and my sister, Nikita. Some say those were hard times in Alabama, and it was. However, our parents worked hard to shield us from the era that we grew up in. They were middle-class business owners who loved their little girls. They spoiled us but still kept us grounded with chores and work through the family businesses. It brings a smile to my face, reminiscing on the good times.

Now, don't get me wrong: there were also some "adventurous" times that left ugly scares, but I thank God for the good and the bad that continue to shape me into the woman I am today. I would say I regret some of it but, if I did, I may not be me—and I like me! In fact, compared to the rest of the ordeals I would go through in my adulthood, there is much to appreciate about my childhood, upbringing, and time of correction. I would gladly go back to those days, anytime.

But then came the part of my journey that forced me to bend in the midst of the storm but, because of God, I didn't break. So much happened in what seemed like a short amount of time: blatant racism while serving in the United States military, a threatening stalker, domestic violence from my first husband (a military superior and a preacher), divorce, physical challenges in both my children and myself, and the emotional turmoil of surviving the death of loved ones including both my parents, a baby, and my stepbrother, all within twenty-six months of each other. Fast-forward a few years and another round of storms came: more deaths, along with foreclosure, repossession, depression, and PTSD. But God!

Life happens to all of us, but how we handle it or don't handle it determines our emotional state. For a long while, I didn't handle it well at all. I was just going through the motions of getting up and putting one foot in front of the other. My life at the time was like the famous image on the Internet of Jesus carrying the woman on the seashore, leaving a trail of His footprints in the sand. I know that He is the only way I made it through the days. I knew I had to be strong, but I had no strength, so I would cry out for God to help me and hide my emotional state from my husband and friends. After all, no one could bring my parents back, no one could bring my baby back, no one could bring my Godfather back, and on and on.

Allow me to share a little bit more about one of those stormy seasons in this life that God so graciously has given me: the death of our baby. Looking at it from the sunny side of the storm, all I can say is, "Wow, wow, wow." The keeping power of God is incredible.

At this time in my life, my sister, Nikita, and I had already experienced our father being murdered, stepbrother being murdered, and our mother being bed-ridden in a vegetative state from a massive heart attack and stroke. I was pregnant while I was serving in the military base in Houston, Texas under a commander who was everything but caring. I experienced what is called Braxton Hicks contractions; all mothers who've experienced them can tell you that they feel like real-time birth contractions. Well, the doctors admitted me in the hospital, stating that they had to place me on bed rest while they attempted to get the Braxton Hicks under control.

One day, while in the hospital, I was on the phone with Nikita. We were cutting up, laughing hard about something silly I'm sure, and I said, "Girl, let me get off this phone before you make me hurt myself." We hung up and I lay back down on the hospital bed. A few moments later, the nurse came in. She adjusted the baby monitor and got a weird look on her face. Soon, there was a swarm of nurses flooding my room. They adjusted the monitor, and poured gel and rubbed my belly in search of the beautiful sound of life. After they checked and checked, they delivered the horrific news: at five-and-a-half months into my pregnancy, there was no heartbeat. They had to induce labor so that I could give birth to my dead child.

I absolutely lost it. I was just an emotion away from needing to be sedated. Though I knew I had God and my husband, at the time, I needed my mom badly; I needed her touch, her words, her presence. But in her state, there was nothing that she could do for me. My dad too was gone, murdered before my sister and I could have the pleasure of seeing him get old. The person who murdered our dad only got five years for this crime.

The doctors told me that they needed to induce labor; well, they did everything medically possible and, for whatever reason, Lil Gary would not come down to the birth canal. Therefore, the doctors told my husband and I that they had done all they could do at the time. I had to be released from the hospital, and they would try again in a few weeks to induce my labor. At that moment, I truly felt that doctor was insane and perhaps the devil himself. Her "medical opinion" demanded that I continue to carry a five-and-a-half-month-old dead baby inside of me?

Once again, I was one emotion away from having a nervous breakdown. I refused to listen to anything this doctor had to say. I requested that the hospital call for Dr. R. Walker, the doctor who delivered my daughter. I knew he was a man of God and I needed that type of care during this time. He came to my bedside and tried to comfort me and explain what was happening. I asked him why they couldn't just do a C-section to take the baby out, and his words were devastating to the core. He said to me, "If we attempt this and any of the amniotic fluid gets into your blood stream, you will die on the table. I'm sorry but we cannot perform a C-section." Though he was apologetic, he agreed that they would have to release me from the hospital.

I was heartbroken and no one could comfort me. On top of that, the insensitive commander who I mentioned earlier called to inquire when I would be returning to work since I was released from the hospital. I could not report for duty in that condition but he didn't care. He threatened to report me as AWOL, which was nothing but sheer harassment. He didn't care that I couldn't comply, emotionally or physically. He only stopped harassing me after my doctor called him and stated that, if anything were to happen to me, she would report him for harassment and interfering in my health and recovery. Thank God for some aid and relief.

Lil Gary died on March 25th, 1988 but it took the second attempt of inducing labor on April 9th 1988 for him to be delivered. He is buried in Texas City, Texas. First, my father was murdered five months after the murder of my brother. Five months after that, my mother suffered a major heart attack and was bed ridden. This happened all while dealing with the divorce from my physically and emotionally abusive first husband, along with the abandonment of being dropped off at the hospital to give birth to my child alone, with no one to care, except for the doctors and nurses, that I just gave birth to such a beautiful, perfect human. It was during these times that I thought God did not exist. I thought there *couldn't* be a God for me to go through all this hell on earth. The war on the inside was real and overwhelming. If it had not been for the Lord Jesus leaving us a comforter, the Holy Spirit, my little child and I would not have made it. He knows all things. Look at this personal note our Heavenly Father left each of us in Psalm 139:7-18 TLB to hold dear and rely on as we go through the pits of life:

> I can *never* be lost to your Spirit! I can *never* get away from my God! If I go up to heaven, you are there; if I go down to the place of the dead, you are there. If I ride the morning winds to the farthest oceans, even there your hand will guide me, your strength will support me. If I try to hide in the darkness, the night becomes light around me. For even darkness cannot hide from God; to you the night shines as bright as day. Darkness and light are both alike to you.

> You made all the delicate, inner parts of my body and knit them together in my mother's womb. Thank you for making me so wonderfully complex! It is amazing to think about. Your workmanship is marvelous—and how well I know it. You were there while I was being formed in utter seclusion! You saw me before I was born and scheduled each day of my life before I began to breathe. Every day was recorded in your book!

> How precious it is, Lord, to realize that you are thinking about me constantly! I can't even count how many times a day your thoughts turn toward me. And when I waken in the morning, you are still thinking of me!

Whew, isn't that good? It's so comforting to know how special we are in Him. He has a proven track record. He is always with us.

Yes, I was a wreck so many times in my earlier life. But I know without a shadow of a doubt that it was my root system and the way He created us—just like how He created the palm trees to withstand storms—that kept me secure in God and in myself! You and I are built to withstand all that life throws at us. Philippians 2:13 AMP proclaims, "For it is [not your strength, but it is] God who is effectively at work in you, both to will and to work [that is, strengthening, energizing, and creating in you the longing and the ability to fulfill your purpose] for His good pleasure." Thirty years of marriage (Oct 2017); Praise God; four children, four grandchildren thus far, a ministry of the Gospel, Inspirational Speaker, a successful commercial cleaning business and a striving community focus nonprofit. But God.

1 Peter 5:10 TLB declares, "After you have suffered a little while, our God, who is full of kindness through Christ, will give you his eternal glory." He will personally come to pick you up, set you firmly in place, and make you stronger than ever.

The storms and hurricanes of life are real but so is your strength. He will make your comeback amazing. You can win against all odds.

Believe this: you are a palm tree and you are stronger than you think!

RELAX AND RESET
Escaping from the Grasp of a Predator

....

Cynthia E. Rodgers

By way of introduction, I am a former failure. I have made a series of errors, mistakes, and bad decisions. I have self-inflicted innumerable wounds based on my infatuation with that which looks appealing, smells enticing, sounds promising, feels pleasing, and tastes divine. I am Cynthia E. Rodgers, aficionado of destructive behaviors and close acquaintance to fumbles and setbacks. I am the girl from Alabama who embodies the curiosity of the Missourian—you must show, not tell me. Trial and Error have served as my schoolmasters and I've graced stages and platforms throughout this nation, lovingly disclosing the outcomes of my sense-driven living.

I'm a motivational, thought-provoking speaker by training. I've invested seventeen years (and counting) of my life at the University of Alabama in Birmingham, serving underserved women, infants, children, and youth living with and affected by HIV/AIDS. My position provides insight and viable strategies to people who have been traumatized by series of unfortunate events. I provide an escape route to freedom for those enslaved to chaos. If you feel as though your life is being held hostage by a gun-wielding captor who refuses to let go—be it person, place, or thing—, I want to teach you how to escape him with your freedom.

Let's take a look at the animal kingdom: picture in your mind a stealthy gazelle running through the jungle, clocking nothing less than eighty miles per hour. This beautiful creature, known for its speed, has detected danger in her periphery. She has found herself no longer freely scampering about in her habitat. She is now a prey on the run from a hungry lioness. The lioness is merely on her quest to satisfy the needs of the pride, but her agenda makes her the predator, the threat to our gazelle's life, liberty, and any other pursuits. The lioness closes in—then the inevitable pounce followed by a death grip between the salivating jowls of the captor. Imagine the surreal thoughts flooding the gazelle's mind: "How did I end up here?" "What did I do to deserve this?" The wondering then gives way to, "How the heck am I going to get out of this one?" Any of this sound familiar?

I was sitting in my bedroom on my twin bed at the innocent age of seven years old. I was watching television when a family member entered my bedroom and made an inquiry of my entertainment choice. Then, without warning, he slipped his adolescent tongue into my mouth. I didn't understand the violation, so I didn't resist. My seven-year-old self didn't perceive violation or danger. I merely acquiesced to his charge.

Days of grooming would follow throughout the next year whenever he'd come over for family gatherings or to babysit me. Then, without warning, he pounced! It was Christmas vacation. My mother came to retrieve me from the last day of school, and our family caravanned north to gather for the holidays with my mother's siblings. I asked my mother if Santa Claus would be able to find me even with our absence from home this year—she eased my anxiety and guaranteed that our family trip would not confuse or disrupt the delivery of my presents.

The town was covered in snow. My family celebrated with food, fun, and winter festivities. As the evening progressed, I retreated to the guest room to which my parents and I were assigned. I crawled into that big bed with sounds of loud music and laughter behind the closed door. I drifted off to sleep but was soon awakened by the predator's appetite. I, the second grader at Christmas with her family, was the gazelle, the prey caught in the jowls. How did I end up here? What did I do to deserve this? How the heck am I going to get out of this one?

Trauma is painful because of the loss and devastation, but *traumatic* because of its inherent element of surprise. The ambush, the violent takeover, is what incapacitates us. I returned home to Alabama to find Santa's presents, just as my mother promised. But I honestly wished she would've warned me instead that this second grader would not return home the same. I had no idea how that joyous holiday gathering with my parents, aunts, uncles, and family friends would be the stone that would cause a rippling effect in my life for many years to come.

This episode took place over forty years ago and I'm reliving it to encourage you. Dearest friend, there is no circumstance that can hold you captive as its prey. You can escape the jaws of death, and live! The traumatic experience of molestation is a daunting foe to battle and conquer. The accusatory questions we ask ourselves, the self-interrogation, creates a quagmire of guilt, shame, and blame, alongside a host of counterproductive behaviors and attitudes that stunt our growth and development. But have no fear, friend—don't you dare be dismayed. There's hope for us!

Let's go back to our gazelle: she is locked in the chops of the predator. If the gazelle is going to flee impending doom, two things must happen: the prey has to 1) relax and 2) reset. I know you're probably thinking, "How can I relax when I'm facing a devourer? That doesn't even sound logical!" Trust me, friend, I'm telling you what I've witnessed and experienced over the years. There is an over-confidence and invincibility that every predator feels when it looks like his or her power is at its height. However, if you can endure the temporary discomfort while simultaneously strategizing your great escape, freedom will be yours!

As it happened, my predator was my caregiver for a particular evening. I remember the dance was about to begin, but this time, the outcome would be different. He eclipsed me in a narrow hallway that lead to my bedroom. Face to face and absent of fear and submission, I relaxed and reset: I said, "If you touch me again, I'm going to tell Grandmamma." No drama. No big production. No tears. No fear. I calmly and resolutely posed the ultimatum.

To which he replied, "What makes you think she will believe you?"

Now, I don't know how I mustered the chutzpah to stand up to him, but I did. Without hesitation, I retorted, "Who do you think they'll believe? Big old you or little me?" Baby, that joker never approached me again! I wiggled my way out of the jaws of a man-eating beast and lived to tell the tale.

Listen, I'm no different than you are. I have no magic, no mojo, or no superhuman strength. God endowed me with the ability to relax after that initial traumatic occurrence during Christmas. He allowed my mental faculties to then reset from victim to victor. I have to give Him the honor that He deserves because there's absolutely no way I could have confronted the predator that evening without His will. Even now, when challenged by the threat of danger or trauma, I strong-arm myself to get to a relaxed state of mind. I try to police my emotions because, whenever I allow my emotions to take control, I can't hear directions or instructions. It's the quiet spirit that is able to receive comfort and insight. If I can hear from God, my Source, I can reset. If I can regroup from the attack, I'll then conquer!

There's a scripture I love that says, "Why are you in despair, O my soul? And why have you become restless and disturbed within me? Hope in God and wait expectantly for Him, for I shall again praise Him for the help of His presence" (Psalm 42:5). Dearest friend, in the presence of chaos, you must speak peace to your spirit. Remember the scripture that speaks of when Jesus and His disciples are hit by a violent storm while on a mission: Jesus was asleep while the team was losing it. They awakened him with their fear and he calmly yet assertively spoke to the violent storm and it ceased. Again, I must reiterate: I'm not superhuman and, yes, sometimes I take the harness off of my emotions and squeal and run about like a pig on the third of July! But it never ends well when I freak out. If I can settle down to a warm simmer, I can get instructions from above, and answers and strategies will come to me.

I've shared a prism in the crystal of my colorful life with the hope that you will not feel isolated and powerless between the jaws of a predator. You may be in a tumultuous relationship that is plagued by violence. You may deeply love someone who has a death grip on you, wraps him or herself around you and sucks the life, hopes, and dreams out of you like a python squeezes its prey. I'm here to tell you that you can escape and live as the survivor, the victor, and the conqueror! Don't waste your energy fighting and blaming yourself. And for goodness sakes, don't squander your time and beauty by becoming bitter. Speak to your spirit to quiet down so that you can receive the guidance and instruction to relax and reset.

By no means am I trivializing or minimizing the effects of our traumatic experiences with a two-step process. I understand the debilitating effects of physical, sexual, or mental abuse. I inflicted so much pain upon myself because of my distorted self-image. I used to believe my purpose on this planet was to please others, sexually or financially. I figured the only thing I could do to be loved and accepted was to give whatever was required of me with a pleasant attitude and a smile. I was sadly and erroneously mistaken.

I am one Black woman who can attest to the necessity and effectiveness of accessing mental health treatment. I reached out to a psychotherapist for my doggone self and I spent nearly four years unearthing painful memories, recurring fears, repeated negative images, and everything that needed to be taken down in the fight for freedom. Lord knows I'm better because of the tools I received from my therapist. I also saw a psychiatrist who prescribed a much-needed antidepressant to help a sister out as I worked through the trauma! I'm unashamedly grateful for the process that I embarked upon years ago. There's nothing wrong with getting help.

I've tried my darnedest to articulate my divinely inspired method for escaping a predator. I want you to know that no person, place, or thing can continue to hold you captive without your permission. My heart's desire is that you reach a revelation of how powerful you really are. And finally, always remember that there is a Sovereign and Adoring Heavenly Father Who has brought you through horrendous traumatic experiences.

My darling friend, there's more to life than survival—there's healing and wholeness available to you. You can win against all odds. Welcome to the first day of your comeback. Pray this prayer with me:

Heavenly Father,

I've been hurt. I thought, if You loved me, You wouldn't allow someone to take advantage of me. I still don't understand why it happened to me. Please give me the understanding, power, and ability to be free from the trauma that scared the heck out of me! I want to be free. I want to be whole. I want to experience Your Divine love and I want to love in return. I need You. Please allow my heart to trust You again. In the matchless name of Jesus, I pray!

Amen

AFTER TRAGEDY COMES TRIUMPH

Katrina Seals

I am no longer intimidated by the rejected person I see in the mirror. I am no longer living in fear of low self-esteem. I now know the person I was created to be. I'm a unique masterpiece created for God's use. I am beauty, I am love, and I am whole!

I am going to tell you a story about a little girl from Alabama, whose tragedy always seemed to outweigh the triumph in her life. A girl who was rejected, misunderstood, and blinded by all the cloudy disturbances of life around her. Yes, you guessed it: that little lost girl was me. Rejection is a powerful and painful thing. But you do not have to be held hostage to its mental, physical, and emotional pain!

Born the only child to teenage parents, I had the biggest heart, aimed to please my family and friends. My first encounter with rejection came from the person most of you run to for comfort: my father. I longed for a relationship with him, but all I was ever presented with was broken promises, disappointment, and hurt over and over again. My mom tried her best to fill that void and to provide for me the best she knew how, but the desire to have a relationship with my dad always outweighed any and everything. I spent years searching for my identity, wondering who I could identify myself with. The only thing I wanted was to be loved and accepted. Was that too much to ask?

Years passed and my experience with rejection became second nature to me. My father's rejection of me ultimately caused a lot of confusion and eternal wounds: it made me believe that no one would ever want. At the time, I never acknowledged my feelings, so I simply believed that I could only live my life through rejection and anything other than that was simply not right or undeserved. Why would anyone love me? Why should anyone care about me? I sincerely believed this about myself, so I always put a big smile on my face, even though I was dying on the inside from the constant teasing and isolation I experienced from those around me. There were even times when family members didn't even want to be around me all because they didn't like the church my mother and I attended. What a joke!

By the time I became a pre-teen, my self-esteem was at zero. All that pain and rejection opened up negative doors all around me and continued to create more disappointments. It changed my life for the worst in so many ways. I found myself doing things to make people like me and to feel accepted and love by "friends" who only hung around me to take what I could offer them without giving back. I became so vulnerable and abused that I lost who I really was. It was as if everyone knew so well that they could use me to gain what they wanted, but had no idea that they were causing more hurt to build up in me. I was a marionette, tied up by strings, being lead through life by rejection, loneliness, hurt, and disappointment. I barely existed.

I began to believe that true love and real friendship didn't exist. When you've experienced so much in your life, you're pretty much blinded by everything. I wanted to be loved so badly that I eventually started looking in all the wrong places to receive that love. Yes, the first man who acted as if I was the only thing in the world that could make him happy and said that he "loved" me with everything in him, I melted at his feet. Correct thing to do, right? Wrong! I became engulfed in the attention I received from him. If he would have asked me to jump off a bridge, I would've said, "You want me to jump later or right now?" It's funny how you can sit and reminisce on some of the dumb and silly stuff you did. Thank God, I can laugh about it now.

This was really a trying part of my life. I became a first-time mother at the tender age of fifteen. The only support I had at this point was my family. Day after day, I was constantly ridiculed by my child's paternal family. It left me feeling completely broken. At sixteen, I became pregnant again by another man. This time, because of all the verbal abuse I received from my first child's family, I had an abortion. What was I supposed to do with a seven-month-old daughter and newborn? How was I supposed to make it with two babies? I was barely a young adult and my daughter's father and family were already out of the picture—I thought that this new man and his family were going to do exact same thing. But that abortion was the worst decision I made in my life. My insides felt empty, as if every ounce of blood left my body. I died that day, alongside my baby. That pain is a pain I wouldn't wish on my worst enemy.

Two years later, I met my husband when I was eighteen years old. Things were destined to get better now. I mean, he married me! Surely the love I wanted so badly was coming from him! He's my husband, so of course he loves me more than life itself! Well, he does, but it didn't start off that way. That storm came in fast with winds at 1,000,000,000 mph from every direction! We have to remember that all roses have thorns.

I married my husband when I was nineteen years old. In 1997, we suffered the death of our first son. God blessed us with another son in 1998. Throughout my marriage, I suffered miscarriage after miscarriage, however, God continued to bless my husband and I with four living children. As if this devastation wasn't bad enough, after three years of marriage, I soon learned that my husband was addicted to drugs and unfaithful to me. Suddenly, it made sense that he was being verbally and mentally abusive towards me. Still, I did everything in my power to hide our problems from my family. The storm just grew and grew.

In 1999, I decided it was time for a fresh start in our lives. I moved to Florida thinking, "This is exactly what my family needs!" Well, I can admit that, for the first year, everything was wonderful. I was beginning to see those roses in my husband without the thorns. But then, the thorns reared their most pointed tips yet! My husband continued his drug abuse and his addiction got bigger and bigger. He would leave the kids and me for days at a time. Every time he walked out that front door, he caused me so much pain and disappointment.

I often asked myself, "Girl, how are you supposed to make it?," but I stayed loyal and faithful to my husband. I couldn't give up on "For Better or Worse." I tried to help him as best as I could. Day after day, I tried and tried, often time running to dead-end roads. You see, my husband was not willing to accept that he had a problem, and there was really nothing I could do.

From 2002 to 2003, my kids and I became homeless. Most nights, we slept in the car without any food to eat. Even in my biggest storm, there was always an inkling of light at the end of the tunnel. God allowed me to be able to feed my kids through my employer. There were some nights I couldn't feed myself, but at the end of the day, my kids were able to eat and that in and of itself gave me joy. Still, I had to face the fact that I had lost everything I owned. That's when I knew something had to give.

In 2005, I made my transition in life. I moved back to Alabama to take care of unfinished business and start my life over, but not before being betrayed by someone very, very close to me. By this time, it was no secret that I had suffered through many trials. I was damaged goods. My past had me so broken, and I was emotionally and physically handicapped by the pain of rejection. Now, throughout all this, God was with me. He sustained me. I just couldn't see Him through all the hurt, rejection, and the disappointments, couldn't feel Him walking with me the whole time.

But one day, I was able to see a ray of light when I completely broke down and cried. I asked the Lord, "God, how much more can I take? I'm broken, God, and there's nothing else I can do. I need you. Help me, please. I'm at my breaking point and I'm ready to give up!" Just after I spoke those words, a peace overtook my body. I knew from that moment forward that I could make it.

In 2009, God placed a special person in my life: Pastor Annette Dunner of Mustard Seed Faith Cathedral. This amazing person gave me Godly counsel without judging or treating me less than God's child. I shared everything with her and she gave me clarity. She helped me see that, even though I suffered a whole lot, I was not innocent either. Yes, I was a victim, but I also created victims as well. She stayed up with me all night as I told her about all the wrong that I'd done and all the pain I suffered. She always told me what was right and everything that was true, no matter if it hurt my feelings or not. After our talks, which were often hard and raw, she still showed me love and fed me. Man, does that lady know how to cook!

Even after I told Pastor Dunner the most shameful things I had done throughout my life, she never once looked at me differently, even to this day. She continues to encourage me to fulfill my purpose in God. From day one, I accepted her counsel because I wanted to get to the root of my pain. I wanted real change in my life—rather, I *deserved* a new beginning in my life! Not just a natural beginning—a spiritual one, as well. Yes, I still wanted to be loved, but at this point in my life, I wanted to be happy and free of the bondage that came with *needing* to be loved no matter what. I was ready to accept my freedom and to walk in my freedom. I made a vow to do just that.

I surrendered my life to God and allowed Him to turn my life around. He restored my life abundantly and I thank Him for keeping my family and me safe through the many trials we faced. I am now a business owner, my marriage is restored, my husband is no longer an addict (God delivered Him from drugs!), and mended my family back together! He continues to work things out for us. I would could go on and on about how God protected me.

To those who read this chapter, there is hope. It doesn't matter who you are, what you've done or where you've been, you can come back to life! You must be willing to change, acknowledge, and face both the good and the bad in your life. You must have the desire to tackle the root of your problems, no matter how far you have to dig. The road to recovery is never easy, but the resulting peace, love, and happiness is well worth every tear shed on your journey. When you are able to acknowledge your failures and admit your faults, the freedom you experience is precious and priceless. If I had never experienced all the hurt in my life, I wouldn't have ever known the person God destined me to be.

Jeremiah 29:11 states "'I know the plans I have for you,' declares the Lord, 'plans to prosper you and not harm you, plans to give you hope and a future.'" This plan is not just for me—it's for you too. I am Katrina Seals, broken but never forgotten! My triumph is now! You can win against all odds.

YOUR LATTER CAN BE GREATER THAN YOUR FORMER YEARS

Dee Edwards

The very first time I laid eyes on her, it was love at first sight. In my eyes, she was a Cover Girl. She had a huge, beautiful, contagious smile that lit up a room. She was the right height, the right size; and she exuded confidence that was very attractive. She didn't notice me, but I noticed everything about her. I sat back and admired the way she moved through the club and made everyone feel as if they were superstars. She had that "It" factor.

Should I go up to her or should I wait for her to approach me? I wasn't sure how to act since this was my first time in a gay club and the first time I saw a woman who made me feel butterflies in my stomach in a way that I'd never experienced. All I could do was sit enviously, wishing it was me who she was looking seductively as she danced with a young, beautiful woman on the stage. I had to figure out a way to get her to notice me.

Then all of a sudden, my song came on. I jumped to my feet and started swaying my hips from side to side. Before I knew it, I was on the stage with a cup in my hand, dancing right behind this beautiful woman. She was still dancing with the other young lady, who I later discovered was her girlfriend. In the moment we made eye contact, I almost froze up, but I mustered the courage to slide my number into her pocket with one hand while I held my drink in another, trying not to look too suspicious and to avoid any eye contact with her girlfriend. I danced away as if I had won a championship game—I didn't know that what I had done and my eagerness to get to know her was the very thing that was going to change my life forever.

I waited an entire week for her to call me but she never did. Still, I was determined to get to know her. For the next few weekends, I went to the club every Saturday just to see her even if she didn't say a word to me. I tried to have a good time with my friends, but I couldn't concentrate. I was trying to find that perfect moment to bump into her or even catch her alone. But she was always with the same young lady I saw her with the first night. Sometimes, I would find myself just sitting and staring at her while visualizing us alone. In my mind, she would stare right back at me, even though we would never say one word to each other.

One night, I finally caught her in the club by herself—it was my time to finally make the move that I had been waiting, planning, and yearning to make. I slipped into the small space beside her as she sat down to take a break from dancing. To break the ice, I asked about the whereabouts of her girlfriend. I really didn't care where she was, but I was trying to get a feel for her since this was my first time actually talking to her.

I knew immediately that she liked something about me from the way she looked at me. We danced and talked, and the moment she told me that she loved my eyes, I knew I had her. Checkmate! As the club was beginning to close, we hugged and exchanged numbers. Still to this day, I can't remember if she called me first or if I called her, but after that night, we talked on the phone as if we had known each other for years. Our conversations flowed naturally and she understood me. After spending hours on the phone with her one particular day, I finally asked about her relationship. I was surprised to find out that she and her partner lived together, but she had recently left to go out of town.

I soon convinced her to let me drive up from Tuscaloosa to meet her and her kids in Birmingham. We had that undeniable chemistry as we laughed and talked like one big happy family. We were the same way in person as we were on the phone. There was definitely an attraction.

By the end of the day, she didn't want me to leave and I didn't want to either, but I had to return to my apartment and life. Besides, I knew that her girlfriend would be home soon. She and I continued to talk on the phone, and I found myself really falling for this woman who was at least thirteen years older than me with four children. At the time, I lied to her about my age: if she ever found out that I was barely eighteen, straight out of high school with no children, she would not have ever pursued a relationship with me. I knew that I was different because I had been on my own since I was sixteen years old, so I didn't act, think or talk like an eighteen-year-old. I was very mature for my age, but that would not have mattered if she would have found out because she had a daughter who was only a few years younger than me.

Our friendship continued to grow as her relationship with her girlfriend started to deteriorate. By this time, I was traveling back and forth to see her as much as I could. I was spending time with her children and it felt like I was a part of the family. This continued on for a few months. We laughed, talked, and our feelings for each other kept growing, but we never crossed the lines. We just enjoyed each other's conversation and the time we spent together. Then, it happened: she and her girlfriend broke up.

About a month later, I terminated the lease to my apartment and moved to Birmingham to start our life together. She eventually found out how old I was when I actually turned eighteen, but it was too late for us to turn back. We shared an amazing life together. People in the LGBTQ community respected us. The kids were excelling in school. We both had great jobs and we purchased a house together. We had money, motorcycles, and nice clothes. We had it all. Four years later, things were still going strong until we started going to church together.

I had not been to church in years and the first time we went to Agape Missionary Baptist Church, I felt like I came home. This was the time in my life that I really desired to build an authentic relationship with God. I wanted to know Him. One day, I decided to start spending some time reading the Word, but I didn't know where to start or what to read. So, I decided to flip to the back of the Bible and look up scriptures regarding homosexuality. As I was reading, this was the first time I felt convicted about my lifestyle. But when I read the Word for myself, I felt something strange happening to me on the inside. I was second guessing my relationship and wondering if I was making the right decision about my life. Was this the lifestyle I really wanted to live?

I very cautiously asking my partner, "Is this relationship between us wrong? Are we supposed to be doing this?"

She said, "Yes, it is wrong, but God wouldn't have given us these feeling for each other if it wasn't meant to be."

I felt as if my life stopped. I couldn't breathe because all I heard her say was that our relationship with each other was actually wrong. However, I didn't care how wrong it was. I wasn't willing to walk away from her and the comfortable life that we had built with each other. I wasn't ready to start over. So we kept things normal. We continued to go to church together, made future plans, and kept our lives as normal as possible, but I couldn't get that conversation out of my mind. I felt uneasy. I could no longer sit in the church with her with the thought that I was defying God. It was harder for me to look in her eyes with the way I was feeling in my heart. It was wrong. Instead, I decided to visit another church without her. I saw things about me begin to change, but my relationship with my girlfriend stayed the same. Soon, my convictions would no longer keep silent.

One Sunday morning, I woke up feeling as if I was in the valley of decisions. God was telling me that it was time to leave the relationship. Still, I wanted to reason with Him. It was like the Bible scripture in which the Spirit leads Jesus into the wilderness for forty days and forty nights to be tempted by the devil. I imagined seeing the devil standing at the top of a mountain with his arms stretched wide, telling Jesus that this world could be His if He would bow down and worship him.

I felt as if God was giving me an ultimatum. I had the devil on one side telling me that I shouldn't give up all that my girlfriend and I had built over the five years we were together, and God on the other side giving me the option to choose Him. I honestly didn't know what to do. I thought about her kids who I loved as my own, and all the things we had done and accomplished together. Above all, I loved her. She loved me. She helped me accomplish goals I never thought I could. She was the first person who ever believed in me, the reason that my life was on the right path, the reason that I came back to church. She taught me just about everything I knew. I couldn't believe that God wanted me to leave the one person who didn't give up on me.

I went to church that morning and told God that if I didn't receive word or clarity from Him I would not leave her. By the time I got to church, I was broken. I was in tears. I couldn't concentrate on the message. I was overwhelmed at the thought of what my life would be without her and I was scared. During altar call, I walked to the front of the church with tears streaming down my face as the intercessor stood there, waiting to pray for me. When she asked for my prayer request, I was crying so hard I couldn't say a word. As I stood there in tears, unable to speak, the intercessor said, "The decision that you are making is the right decision."

After hearing those words, I broke down. I was crying and screaming, and I couldn't stop. God really heard my prayers. I was about to make a decision that would change the entire course of my life. She said again, "God really wants you to know that you're making the right decision." I couldn't stop crying as the ushers had to help me back to my seat. The young lady at the altar followed me to my seat and spoke those words to me again: "God really wants you to know that you're making the right decision." I continued to sob: I didn't realize until later that I was actually mourning the loss of my relationship with my soon-to-be ex-girlfriend. God just wanted me to know that it was time to end what I thought was going to be a lifetime commitment.

When I went home that day, I knew I had to tell my girlfriend that I was leaving her to make my relationship with God right. It wasn't because I didn't love her; I just wanted to obey God. Surprisingly, she wasn't angry with me. She had started to see the change in me and, looking back, I knew that God was preparing her heart for our breakup. She was hurt that I was leaving and so was I. It felt like I was letting her and the kids down because we planned to spend the rest of our lives together. That night, we lay in bed, trying to comfort each other as we cried ourselves to sleep. I tried to fight my sleep, because I knew that the next morning, my life would change permanently. I would leave everything behind. I couldn't take the old life with me. My thinking had to change. My environment had to change. My friends had to change. All because I was changing. I was being made new the very moment I decided to walk away for the glory of Him. I didn't know my next move or how I was going to survive without her. I just knew that I had to do it. It was time for me to start all over again.

What I learned from my own life's experiences is that, oftentimes, you must make a move in faith without having all of the answers. God wants to know if you will obey and trust Him to walk into the unknown, and sometimes, that means starting from scratch. It was difficult for me to start from ground zero while everyone else seemed to elevate in their lives. At one point, I had to live in the basement of my church member's home. I felt abandoned, lonely, and hopeless, but thanks be unto God Who gives us overwhelming victory—after making one of the hardest decisions of my life and going through the process, God restored everything that I left. Everything I gave up, He returned to me and much more.

To experience what God has for you, you must be willing to lose it all. There's a story in the Bible that talks about how God tells Lot to leave his homeland, but, just like me, Lot couldn't see he had to leave familiarity to obtain new promises. I cried many nights during my process and questioned whether I made the right decision or not. I even wanted to be like Lot's wife and look back—but deep down, I knew that my girlfriend came into my life for a purpose and God had used her to bring me to Him. One decision made my crooked road straight and changed the path of my life.

My story isn't about whether or not homosexuality is wrong; instead, I am only trying to exemplify Isaiah 1:19, "If ye be willing and obedient ye will eat the good of the land." Now I have been married to the man of my dreams, Michael A. Edwards, II, Senior Pastor of The Celebration Church, for almost thirteen years. I have amazing children, family, friends, and several thriving and successful businesses. Also, I am a two-time bestselling author.

Who would have known that God was setting me up for a comeback? I don't know where you are in your life or what you may be going through, but don't be afraid to start from scratch. You have to be willing to risk it all and step out of the boat. All God gave Peter was a Word to come to Him when Peter wanted to walk on water. Sometimes, all God will give you is a command. No sign. No confirmation. No explanation. No direction. One word. When I packed up my clothes to leave, I didn't know what the future held, but after knowing the truth, I couldn't stay living comfortably, but being uncomfortable in my Spirit. If I would have stayed in my situation, I would have never known what was waiting for me. I am your example that your latter can be greater than your former years. You can win against all odds.

ABOUT THE AUTHORS

About the Authors

Dee Edwards is a faith-based business leader, entrepreneur, and best-selling author of *10 Mistakes Business Owners Make and How to Avoid Them* and *Belief, Boldness, BIG Blessings*. In 2012, she and her husband, Michael, launched a nationwide tax and financial firm to provide accurate tax preparation and financial services to individuals and small business owners. She has also launched several tax offices in Alabama to include a Latino division and has become the only independently owned continuing education provider with the IRS in Alabama. As founder of the IRS Tax Schooling, Edwards provides training, resources, and coaching to CPAs, enrolled agents, and tax startup business owners. In addition, she is a master business coach and president of The Startup Business Factory, through which she offers coaching, digital products, and workshops that help startup business owners move from idea to execution, gain vision clarity, overcome frustration, and build a profitable and sustainable business. As the visionary of *The Comeback*, it is her heart's desires to give individuals hope to strengthen their faith by gathering a group of women who have gone through various trials.

Contact Dee Edwards at www.DeeEdwardsOnline.com
Email: Dee@DeeEdwardsOnline.com.

Mary Mallory is an author, minister, mother, grandmother, and woman of God. She is a member of True Love Church where she serves on the outreach ministry, God's Secret Weapons (GSW), choir, and the youth ministry. She is a graduate of Herzing College and Birmingham Easonian Baptist Bible College. She is currently attending the Ministry Training Institute at Samford University.

Mallory has been married to Edward Mallory for thirty-nine years. She is a mother of three sons and three daughters-in-law, and a grandmother of three.

About the Authors

Shan Washington was born and raised in Montgomery, Alabama, in a small community called Madison Park. With a background in banking and hospitality, she became an entrepreneur in 2010 through founding her tax office, S&Z Tax Service. Since its opening, S&Z Tax Service now services multiple states in the East South Central and South Atlantic area. Meanwhile, Shan has opened several other businesses, including a women's boutique store named Platinum Dollz Studio and a party entertainment service named B3 Venue, both located in Montgomery.

Shan currently resides in Wetumpka, Alabama, with her son and daughter.

Learn more at platinum.dollz@yahoo.com.

Melissa F. Williams is an author, conference and keynote speaker, and woman of God. She is also the CEO and founder of Melissa Williams Ministry, Daughters of Destiny Inc., The Youth EMPOWERMENT Outreach & Mentoring program, and The Empowerment Learning Academy.

She is also the bestselling author of *Doubt and Destiny Don't Mix* and *After This*.

Williams is the proud mother of three children, Cornelius, Dajia, and Angel, who she raises with the same passion, love, and dedication she puts in to her assignment in ministry.

To connect, visit her website at
www.melissaministries.com or
email her at melissawmsministry@gmail.com

About the Authors

Jamika Mays was born in Birmingham, Alabama and grew up in a small neighborhood called Collegeville. Having always had a mind for entrepreneurship, she now owns and operates two successful businesses, Dazzle Her and 3D Tax & Financial Services INC. She has associate of science degrees in medical office management and phlebotomy.

For more information, visit www.dazzleher.net.

Victoria Necole is a mother, daughter, entrepreneur, author, and confidence coach. She the co-owner of the non-profit organization, The Confessions of a Lady, established in August of 2015, and owner of the small business boutique, Delani's, established in September of 2013. She is a victor against domestic violence, sexual abuse, and suicide attempts.

Long is the proud mother of a seven-year-old Kaytlyn "Lady" Delani.

To connect, visit her website at www.victorianlong.com or email her at victoria@victorianlong.com

About the Authors

Mesia Rena is an entrepreneur, motivational speaker, author, and business coach. She has successfully launched the following businesses: Beauty & Curves Boutique, Right on Time Taxes, 2nd Chance Financial Services, Pink Guru Fitness, and Success with Mesia Rena. In addition, she is also a business coach to small business owners, helping them establish, maintain, and grow their businesses.

Mesia Rena is a native of Birmingham, Alabama, and is the wife of Archie Allen.

For more information about Mesia Rena,
visit www.mesiarena.com.

Terria R. Jones is a mentor, motivational speaker, and freelance makeup artist known better as The LifeArtist who helps each of her "effortless beauties" achieve their most phenomenal beauty, inside and out. She is also the voice for her local ministry's announcements as well as an interviewer for their weekly television broadcast. When she is not working or serving, she mentors at several schools in the Birmingham area through D.I.G mentor program, which she co-founded with her husband, Eric Jones.

Jones resides in Birmingham, Alabama with her husband and two children, Ayrika and Morgan.

Starnisha Washington is a business owner, motivational speaker, life coach, and mother. She is the owner of Slimfit Weight Loss Clinics and founder of Luxe Life University, a Business 101 course that gives clients the ends and outs of opening and operating their own businesses. Her goal is to help women take life's circumstances and use them to their advantage to make their dreams a reality.

Learn more at www.iamstarwashington.com

Nicole Johnson is an entrepreneur, financial advisor, and mother. Alongside working for the Social Security Administration, she is also the founder and CEO of B & B Financial Services, through which she teaches her community about responsible financial literacy, budgeting skills, bankruptcy procedures, credit score improvement, home buyer preparation, and more.

Johnson resides in Bessemer, Alabama. She is the mother of two children, Brianna and Brandon.

Connect with her at bandbfinancialservices.org.
Email: nicole@bandbfinanicalservices.org.

Geonisha Brown is an author, financial advisor, entrepreneur in the travel and real estate industries, and a woman of God.

Stacey Yvonne is a business owner, health and wellness specialist, and mother. Alongside working for the Social Security Administration, she is also the owner of KWU's Health & Wellness LLC. She received her personal training certification and fitness and exercise certification from Ashworth College in 2012, as well as her yoni steam certification for womb massage and yoni steam certification in 2017. She is currently in the process of earning her colon hydrotherapy license with IACT.

Yvonne resides in Forestdale, Alabama with her children.

Learn more at www.kwuhealthandwellness.com
Email: stacey@kwushealthandwellness.com

Crystal M. NeVille is a passionate speaker, visionary, business owner, and executive director of the Speak Life Empowerment Nation, a nonprofit, multi-cultural stress relief and empowerment organization in the Birmingham metro area.

Neville is a nine-year veteran of the United States Coast Guard and has been married to her husband, Gary NeVille, since 1987. She is a mother of four adult children and a grandmother of four.

Cynthia E. Rodgers is an orator, writer, national motivational speaker, entertainer, and servant of God. Since September of 2000, she has been dedicated to the mission and vision of The Family Clinic at the University of Alabama in Birmingham, where she as a linkage and retention coordinator. In her role, she provides case management services, HIV treatment, adherence counseling, and psychosocial support services for the retention of patients in care.

Rodgers is a mother of three amazing sons.

Katrina Seals is an entrepreneur, devoted wife, and mother. She is the founder of Seals Enterprise and owner of Five Star Tax and Accounting in Birmingham, Alabama. Before entering the field of finance, she worked in healthcare for sixteen years.

Seals currently resides in Dixiana, Alabama. She earned her certificate in small business management from Brown Mackie College and is currently earning her bachelor's degree in accounting from the University of Ashford. When she is not working, she enjoys spending time with family and friends, attending church, shopping, and taking road trips with her husband.

Learn more by emailing Katrina at
katrinalseals@gmail.com

CREATING DISTINCTIVE BOOKS
WITH INTENTIONAL RESULTS

We're a collaborative group of creative masterminds with a mission to produce high-quality books to position you for monumental success in the marketplace.

Our professional team of writers, editors, designers, and marketing strategists work closely together to ensure that every detail of your book is a clear representation of the message in your writing.

Want to know more?
Write to us at info@publishyourgift.com
or call (888) 949-6228

Discover great books, exclusive offers, and more at
www.PublishYourGift.com

Connect with us on social media

@publishyourgift

www.ingramcontent.com/pod-product-compliance
Lightning Source LLC
Chambersburg PA
CBHW070107120526
44588CB00032B/1309